Extended RV Travel

How To Travel In Your RV For Weeks Or Months At A Time

Revised and Expanded Edition

by Joe and Vicki Kieva

Extended RV Travel

How To Travel In Your RV For Weeks Or Months At A Time

By Joe and Vicki Kieva

Published by RV Travel Adventures
P.O. Box 5055, Huntington Beach, CA 92615
www.rvknowhow.com

All rights reserved. No part of this book may be reproduced, stored or transmitted in any form or by any mechanical or electronic means without prior written permission from the publisher.

Copyright © 1998, 2001 and 2005 by Joe and Vicki Kieva
First Printing 1998
Second Printing 2001, revised
Third printing 2005, revised and expanded
Printed in the United States of America

ISBN # 0-9655620-6-9

The purpose of this book is to educate and entertain. It is designed to provide information about the subject matter covered. Every effort has been made to make this book as accurate as possible. However, there may be mistakes both typographical and in content. Therefore this book should only be used as a guide and not as the ultimate source of RV related information. Safe and responsible use of all vehicles and their attendant equipment is the obligation of the user. The authors and publishers shall have neither liability not responsibility to any person or entity with respect to any loss or damage caused or alleged to be caused directly or indirectly by the information contained in this book. If you do not wish to be bound by the above, you may return this unread book to the publisher for a full refund.

Introduction

In 1974 we made a dream come true. We left our jobs; pulled three kids out of school; loaded up a 17-foot travel trailer and began a five-month tour of North America.

We camped in national parks, toured the Smithsonian Institute and visited an endless number of tourist attractions.

We came home thoroughly addicted to extended RV travel. Never again would a two or three-week vacation satisfy our wanderlust. We changed our lifestyle to accommodate at least one six-to-eight week trip every year.

In 1989 we made another dream come true. We left our jobs so we could devote even more time to RV travel.

Today we spend two to three months at a time on the road. Between trips we return to our house in California. It only takes a month or two, though, before wanderlust gets the best of us and we are on the road again.

During our travels we present seminars at RV shows, rallies and other events. We also write for RV magazines.

Judging by the questions we get from those who attend our seminars and read our columns, there are a lot of RVers who are interested in becoming extended travelers.

This book is an attempt to answer the questions most frequently asked about extended RV travel.

We hope this book will help you make your dreams come true. Be careful, though, you too may succumb to the lure of the open road and find yourself addicted to the joys of extended RV travel.

Enjoy The Journey!

Contents

Start RVing Now	1
Fulltiming Strategies	6
Choosing An RV For Extended Travel	13
Slideout Rooms	22
Microwave/Convection Ovens	27
Clothes Washer/Dryers	31
Switching From Gas To Diesel	35
About Diesel Fuel	41
Choosing A Tow Vehicle	46
Dinghy Towing	49
Home Security And Maintenance	55
Banking And Bill Paying	59
Receiving Mail	64
Medical Care And Prescriptions	68
Telephone Communications	73
Second Cellphone Solution	78
Computers and RVs	81
E-Mail and Internet Connections	84
Office On The Road	89

Contents

What To Take	93
Trip Planning	98
Selecting Campgrounds	103
Locating Uncrowded Campgrounds	108
Membership Campgrounds	110
Self-Contained Camping	115
Cold-Weather Camping	121
Locating Dump Stations	126
Safety and Security	128
Guns N' RVs	135
Traveling With Pets	139
RV Travel Tips	142
Washing The RV	145
Watch The Truckers	147
Trucker Talk	150
Interpreting The Interstates	154
Visiting Big Cities	158
Alaska – Caravan Or Solo?	161
Making Money On The Road	165
Missing The Grandchildren	173
Familiar Places	176
Information To Go	178

Extended - Stretched out, continued or prolonged.

RV - Vehicle providing mobile living accommodations.

Traveler - One who goes from place to place.

Extended RV Traveler - One who goes from place to place in an RV for prolonged periods of time.

Start RVing Now

"I'm retiring in four years and when I do, I'm going to sell my house, buy an RV and be a full-time RVer."

Joe: We hear that dream expressed all the time. Unfortunately, the dreamer is often a person who has no RVing experience whatsoever. He doesn't know anything about the lifestyle he is planning to enter. He just hopes it will be an escape from the way of life he has built for himself over the last 30 or 40 years.

Now, don't get me wrong. A good number of people with no RVing background have retired or quit their jobs and successfully joined the ranks of those who live and travel full time in their RVs. Some have even written educational and entertaining books about their experiences.

We haven't seen many books, though, by those whose dreams were shattered because they bought the wrong RV or by those who spent a lot of money just to learn they were not cut out for RVing. And how many people have sold their home only to discover that while they enjoy traveling in an RV they prefer living in a house?

Vicki: Here's what we suggest to those who are looking forward to an RVing retirement. Don't wait until you retire. Start now to prepare for the lifestyle you are dreaming about. Buy an RV today. Start RVing now. Use the years before your retirement to learn about RVs, RVing and yourself.

You may discover that you don't want to sell your house and be a fulltimer. You may decide, instead, that extended RV travel is what you prefer to do. You might even learn that RVing is not how you want to spend your retirement after all.

The best way to learn is through experience. So start now. Buy an RV, if you don't already have one. It doesn't have to be new or expensive. Think of it as a training rig. This is the one you will use as a benchmark when you go out to buy your retirement RV. You will recover a portion of its purchase price when you buy the next rig, so look at the difference as an investment in your RV education.

Joe: Buy about a 24 to 26-foot trailer or a 28 to 30-foot motorhome. This is a versatile size. It will fit into most government campgrounds yet is large enough to provide the creature comforts you will want for extended periods of time.

Chances are you'll decide on a larger size vehicle for your retirement rig, but you might also discover that this is more than enough RV for your needs. Either way, you'll learn how to make the most out of the space you have.

You'll want the usual electric (30 amp), water and sewer hookup capabilities. If the RV you buy is pre-wired for cable TV and telephone hookups, all the better.

Some RVers camp self-contained most of the time. Others prefer RV parks with full hookups. Most fall somewhere in between. Get an RV with large self-containment capabilities for your learning experience.

There's no such thing as an RV with enough storage space, especially for extended travelers and fulltime RVers.

Be sure you have adequate closet space, cupboards and drawers.

Outside storage bays should be large enough for tools, folding chairs, a grill and other items you don't want to store inside. A rooftop storage pod can be added to carry lightweight items that you will only use occasionally.

Pay close attention to the weight carrying and towing capacities of your training RV. You want as much net cargo-carrying capacity as possible and you don't want to overload your tow vehicle.

If you decide to get a trailer, be sure you have a properly equipped tow vehicle. This could be your present truck or you can buy a decent used one.

If you choose a motorhome, plan on towing a small, lightweight car. A small used car with manual transmission might be the least expensive route to go.

Remember, the plan is to eventually trade in these vehicles and buy the one(s) that will best satisfy your future interests and needs.

Shopping for, purchasing, equipping and operating your training RV will give you experience. Experience is the best teacher. It gives the test first and the lesson afterwards.

Vicki: Once you have your RV ready to go, go! Start with a shakedown trip to a nearby RV park or campground with full hookups. Spend one full day and night camping self contained and another day and night with full hookups. Try out all the features of your rig. The objective is to discover any problems and then get them corrected before you take any serious trips.

Most people who are close to retirement age are usually in a position to take an occasional three or four days off and may even be entitled to three or four week vacations. Take advantage of these days to spend as much time as possible traveling and camping in your RV.

Go to a new and different campground each trip. Get comfortable with the idea of going into and setting up camp in unfamiliar locations. That's what you will be doing as an RV traveler.

Explore a variety of RV parks and campgrounds. Enjoy the RV resorts. Visit the destination RV parks and campgrounds. Stay overnight in enroute parks. Get familiar with the nationwide chain of KOA campgrounds. Camp in national, state, county and city park campgrounds. Spend an occasional night dry camped in the driveways of out-of-town friends and relatives.

Experiment with long travel days and short travel days. Travel early in the day and get off the road before 3:30 in the afternoon. Travel at night. Experiment. You may be surprised at what you discover.

Pursue your interests and hobbies while on the road. Go fishing. Explore ghost towns. Play golf. Visit flea markets. Follow the races. Visit old friends. Make new ones.

After you and your RV have a little experience, begin taking journeys of two to four months duration. Learn what is involved with actually living on the road.

Use these trips to learn about your RV and RVing. You'll also learn about your personal RVing interests, needs and budget.

Joe: Meanwhile, simplify your everyday life. Start with your home. Who will look after it while you are gone for long periods of time? Who will retrieve and forward your mail? Who can act on your behalf while you are absent? With any luck it will be the same person.

Simplify your yard maintenance. Install sprinklers. Hire a gardener. Replace hard to care for plants with easy care ones.

Simplify your banking and bill paying arrangements. How will you accomplish these chores while you are away from home?

Develop a system of communicating with friends and family while you are on the road. Most extended RV travelers have a cellular phone in their RV, a telephone calling card for use at pay phones, and a telephone answering machine at home for taking messages. Ask the campgrounds you visit what facilities they have for e-mail.

Research. Join RV clubs, attend RV shows, explore RV dealerships, subscribe to RV magazines, read RV books, attend RV seminars, visit with fellow RVers, surf the internet. Learn all you can about the various RVs, RV lifestyles, RV parks, campgrounds, travel destinations and activities.

Vicki: Start now. Become an experienced and knowledgeable RVer. Learn just what your personal interests and needs are.

When retirement time gets closer you'll be able to decide whether you want to be a full-time RVer, an extended traveler, a snowbird, an occasional RV user or a confirmed couch potato.

You'll be in a position to choose the RV that will satisfy your interests and needs. You'll be making an informed decision. Best of all, you'll be taking action to make your dream come true!

6

Fulltiming Strategies

We are thinking seriously about becoming full-time RVers when we retire next year. We bought an RV five years ago and have spent a number of enjoyable weekends and two-week vacations at nearby campgrounds. The idea of getting away and being on perpetual vacation really appeals to us. Where do we begin?

Joe: First, understand that Vicki and I are not full-time RVers. We have not shed ourselves of our stuff. We have not sold our house. We have not moved all our worldly possessions into an RV. We are extended RV travelers. Vicki and I go out on the road for months at a time, return to our house in Southern California, spend a month or two at home, and then we go out on the road again. During the course of a calendar year we spend about seven or eight months traveling, working and living in our motorhome. Originally, we planned on becoming full-time RVers but we discovered that while we love traveling in an RV, we prefer living in a house.

We do, however, have some familiarity with the full-time lifestyle. We live like fulltimers when we are on the road. Many of our closest friends are fulltimers. We have seen a lot of folks make the transition to fulltiming. We have talked with any number of current fulltimers. And, we have watched a good number of fulltimers come in off the road. We have had the opportunity to observe the fulltiming lifestyle first-hand and, at the same time, form conclusions as non-fulltimers.

Vicki: When you become a full-time RVer, you are not going on vacation. You are changing your lifestyle. You are not just dipping your toe in to test the water. You are immersing yourself. You want to do some serious thinking. We would like to suggest that you develop three strategies; an entry strategy, a lifestyle strategy, and an exit strategy.

Your entry strategy is essentially preparation for making the transition from your present lifestyle to a full-time RVing lifestyle.

Do your homework. Research to determine which state will be your residence. Our society demands that you reside somewhere if you want to obtain a driver's license, register your vehicles or vote in an election. You might as well pick a state that is beneficial to your personal situation. Analyze the costs of each state as well as its benefits. A state may not tax income, but it might tax investments and property. It might have a low sales tax but a high vehicle-registration fee. Some states require expensive (and inconvenient) periodic vehicle safety inspections. Health and vehicle insurance premiums can also differ from state to state. Ask full-time RVers why they chose or rejected the states they considered.

Talk to a tax accountant. What effect will your move have on your income tax situation? Talk to an attorney. How will your move from one state to another effect your estate or other legal affairs? Talk to the Escapees RV Club (888-757-2582 or www.escapees.com). It was established as an information and support system for full-time and other serious RVers. They are familiar with the road you are about to travel.

Research the pros and cons of selling your house or keeping it as an investment. Think about what you will do with the proceeds if you do sell. What will you do with your furniture and other possessions? We have observed that many fulltimers eventually return to living in a conventional dwelling. Do your plans consider this possibility?

Becoming a full-time RVer means making certain changes in your lifestyle. It takes time to research the changes and time to implement them. Your entry strategy should prepare you for your new lifestyle

Your lifestyle strategy should identify what you will do as a full-time RVer. Where will you go? When? Why? We have observed that most full-time RVers begin as serious travelers. The first couple of years they move quickly from place to place, never staying in one location for any length of time. Their mindset is still like vacationers. Destination, mileage, and time oriented rather than simply enjoying the journey. Once they have criss-crossed the country a couple of times, however, they begin to slow down and spend more time in the places that appeal to them. This is usually the time when they re-evaluate their lifestyle. Some will continue to travel, although at a more leisurely pace. Many will look for a home base, perhaps a campground, where they can settle in for two or three months at a time between journeys. A few will find a comfortable RV park and take up permanent residence. And others will return to a more conventional dwelling. Your RV lifestyle strategy should be flexible. Recognize and allow for the fact that your interests and circumstances can, and probably will, change as you go down the road.

Your exit strategy is simply a plan or arrangement that permits you to make the change from full-time RVing to a more conventional lifestyle.

We are acquainted with a number of fulltimers who have come in off the road. Some, over the course of a number of years, have slowly evolved from frequent travelers to occasional travelers; to living year-round in an RV park; to moving into a conventional dwelling. Others have suddenly found themselves in a position where their personal circumstances forced them to leave the full-time lifestyle entirely. Obviously, the transition was a lot smoother for those who were psychologically and financially prepared.

Joe: Your entry strategy should include spending as much time as possible in your RV before making the move to fulltiming. Longer trips will help you evaluate your present RV's suitability for fulltiming. Is it small and agile enough to take you where you want to go? Is it big enough to carry all your worldly possessions and to provide the creature comforts you require? Is it durable enough to handle the wear and tear of full-time living and long-distance travel? You might discover that your present RV, while it was great for weekends and vacations, is not going to satisfy your full-timing needs.

Longer trips can be used to research and test your arrangements for banking, bill paying, internet service, cell phone service, obtaining medical care, getting prescriptions refilled, and receiving mail.

Trips of longer duration will also help determine if you and your spouse are ready for the full-time lifestyle.

Home owners will be faced with the decision of what to do with their home. If they keep it, what do they do with it? If they sell it, what do they do with the proceeds? For some, the proceeds from the sale will be used to purchase an RV and help finance their transition to fulltiming. For others, keeping the house or investing the profits of its sale provides an income stream and becomes part of their exit strategy.

Your lifestyle strategy - what you will do and where you will go - can be anything you want. That's one of the joys of fulltiming. As Vicki mentioned, most new fulltimers take advantage of their open-ended calendar by traveling. They go to all the places their previous time-constrained lives prevented them from visiting. Some travel with a purpose. They have places to go, things to do, and people to see. Others travel aimlessly, just to sightsee. A number of full-time RVers use their travels to locate the perfect retirement community. Many fulltimers, after a couple of carefree years, return to the work world. Some start on-the-road businesses. Others find temporary or part time jobs. A good number become volunteers. Whatever they do, they seem to choose an activity that satisfies their need to be useful or productive, yet allows them to remain in their RV.

Your lifestyle strategy should be flexible. It is just a starting point. Your lifestyle will change as you observe and experience what the open road has to offer. You will evolve as you go down the road.

Your exit strategy simply takes into consideration that you might not spend the rest of your life living in an RV.

We are acquainted with a number of RVers who became fulltimers with the intention of returning to a more conventional lifestyle when they reached a certain point in life. Most of these folks developed both their entry and exit strategies knowing that, at some time, they would leave the full-time lifestyle.

Most of the full-time RVers we know began as ardent travelers. As the years passed, they seemed to travel less but continued to enjoy the relaxed atmosphere of campgrounds and the camaraderie of other RVers. Some of these folks are now full-time residents of RV parks. Others, while still RV travelers, now live in conventional dwellings.

Our observation is that those who are the most content are the ones who had some kind of exit strategy. Your exit strategy doesn't have to be rigid. But it should provide you with options.

Vicki: All of our full-timing friends love their lifestyle (the ones who didn't, dropped out). They love the sense of self-reliance, the people they meet, and their sense of freedom. You can join them. Do your homework, research, talk to other fulltimers. Develop your entry, lifestyle, and exit strategies. And take time to enjoy the journey!

"For my part, I travel not to go anywhere, but to go. I travel for travel's sake. The greatest affair is to move."

Robert Louis Stevenson

Choosing An RV For Extended Travel

"We want to spend several months each year traveling around the country. What's the best RV for us?"

Joe: Lately, we are hearing that question at almost every RV seminar we present. It would appear that more and more folks are becoming extended RV travelers like us.

Typical extended RV travelers go out in their RV for six to twelve weeks at a time. They may take two or three trips and accumulate 10,000 or more miles a year.

While, essentially, they are on vacation, extended travelers live in their RVs just like fulltimers do. Since they encounter all kinds of weather conditions, their RV wardrobe will range from summer shorts to down jackets and raincoats. It will also include grubbies, casual wear and semi-dressy outfits (with shoes to match).

Extended RV travelers occasionally like to prepare regular home-cooked meals like spaghetti with meat sauce or roast beef and mashed potatoes. They spend more evenings inside their RVs watching television, reading or working on their computer than they do sitting outside next to a campfire.

Extended RV travelers may ask their rigs to climb the Rocky Mountains, cross the southwestern deserts and follow the Alaska Highway. They encounter temperatures from freezing to 120 degrees. Self-containment features are frequently every bit as important as the convenience of hookups.

The ideal rig for an extended RV traveler combines a perfect blend of easy mobility, copious cargo capacity and comfortable living accommodations.

Vicki: The question of whether to get a motorhome or trailer comes first. This is a personal choice with a lot of considerations. Either will do the job.

When we were weekending and vacationing, we had small travel trailers and then a Class C motorhome. They were space efficient, would go anywhere and their price tags were proportionate to the amount of time we spent using them.

If we were to become fulltimers we would give serious consideration to a large conventional or fifth-wheel trailer.

But, as extended RV travelers, we chose a Class A motorhome because it is easy to drive, back and level. That's important when maneuvering in and out of RV parks is almost a daily occurrence.

Class A motorhomes offer comfortable, spacious interiors. Their large outside storage bays are capable of carrying everything we need.

The size of an extended RV traveler's rig is a compromise between interior living comfort and the ability of the RV to fit into the places you want to go. Let's face it, a 40-foot motorhome is more comfortable to live in than a van conversion; the van, however, can go anywhere while the 40- foot motorhome has limitations.

Our personal travels take us to national parks, RV resorts and a variety of commercial and government campgrounds. We have also spent a fair amount of time camped in friends' driveways and the parking lots of RV shows. As a result, we have come to the conclusion that a motorhome between 32 and 36 feet is about the right compromise for our extended RV travel needs.

Joe: Gasoline or diesel? We have driven both gasoline and diesel powered motorhomes across the country. On each of those occasions we were towing a compact car with all four wheels on the ground. This may come as a surprise to many, but we found the performance and capabilities of both the big block V-8 and the 5.9 turbo-charged diesel to be pretty much the same.

The diesel pusher chassis had a significantly higher cargo carrying capacity. It was smoother, quieter, and got better mileage. But the gasoline rig did the job very nicely and the price tag was significantly lower.

The diesel chassis definitely has the advantage when it comes to durability and longevity. If you know you will be extended RV travelers for some time to come. If you think you will put 10,000 miles or more per year on your RV. If your budget can handle the price tag. It makes sense to go with the diesel.

You'll want to tow a small transportation car or truck. Be sure the motorhome is capable of handling the weight.

Extended RV travelers carry lots of stuff. An RV with 3,000 pounds or more of cargo carrying capacity is ideal. Not every RV has this kind of cargo carrying capacity, but they're out there.

One manufacturer, for example, recently introduced an entry level, diesel motorhome with a net carrying capacity of slightly over 5,000 pounds and the capability of towing an additional 5,000 pounds. They also did a dynamite job of weight distribution. Side to side weight variance is less than 250 pounds.

Self-containment capacities are important to extended RV travelers. An 80 to 100-gallon fresh-water tank will provide up to a week's worth of water for two people. An equal size gray-water holding tank is desirable but may not be easy to find.

You'll find that 35 to 40 gallons of black-water holding tank capacity is sufficient for a week of self-contained camping.

We have determined that twin 6-volt batteries, a 2,000 watt inverter and a 6,500 watt generator meet all of our electrical needs while camping self-contained.

A 20 to 25-gallon propane tank will do the job. During really cold weather we have consumed up to a gallon of propane per day; a good deal less during summertime.

A combination gas/electric water heater will save a considerable amount of propane when you have an electric hookup.

Dual pane windows and good insulation will help keep cold weather at bay.

Torque windows in the bedroom will permit cross ventilation when it's raining.

Two roof air-conditioning units, a high-powered roof-vent fan and awnings on all the windows provide relief from the hot sun.

Roof-vent covers make it possible to open the roof vents even though it is raining. We can also drive down the highway with our roof vent open and know the cap won't blow off.

Hydraulic levelers for a motorhome or electric tongue jack for a trailer are real back savers and make leveling and stabilizing an RV faster and easier.

Vicki: RV travelers spend a lot of time inside their rigs. Be sure you get a livable floorplan.

Kitchens located at the front or rear of the rig are usually larger than those located in the center. They also have the advantage of being out of the RV's traffic path.

Many trailer owners have observed that the smoothest riding portion of the trailer is in the front. They prefer to have the kitchen and its breakables located forward of the rear axle.

Rear baths can be large and private but guests sleeping in the front of the RV may disturb the bedroom occupants when they need to use the bathroom.

Split, center baths can also be spacious but may block passage from one end of the RV to the other when they are occupied.

Side-aisle, center baths are accessible from both ends of the RV and don't block traffic, but they frequently are not as spacious as the other plans.

One floorplan offers a compromise by placing the commode and bathroom sink in a small room on one side of the RV and the shower across the hall.

Most RVers appreciate a bedroom that can be closed off from the rest of the RV. It provides privacy for changing clothes and accommodates occupants with different bedtime schedules.

Try the RV on to see if it fits. Sit down in the living area. Would you be comfortable spending an evening in that couch or chair? Are the lights adequate for reading? Where will you place your snack, cold drink and the TV remote control? Is the television easily viewed from every seat?

Convert the couch into a bed. Lie down on both sides. Is it comfortable? A six-foot person would appreciate a bed that is at least 74 inches long. Is the storage area under the couch easily accessible?

A free-standing kitchen table and chairs look homey, are easier to get in and out of and give the RV a spacious appearance. A bench seat dinette, on the other hand, provides under-seat storage, the availability of a guest bed and you don't have to secure any chairs before you travel.

How much countertop is available for meal preparation? A side-by-side refrigerator, icemaker and combination microwave/convection oven are all very nice but you need counter space to prepare a meal and stack dirty dishes.

If the kitchen table is located opposite the kitchen counter, it will be convenient for use during meal preparation.

Kitchen sinks should be deep enough to wash your largest pot. The sinks in some RVs take up more counter top area than in others, yet their usable interior dimensions are the same.

Consider how important a propane oven may be to you. A microwave/convection oven can do the same job as a propane oven but may not be operable when you are camping without electric hookups. If the propane oven isn't important, take the large storage space in its place.

Refrigerator interiors generally seem pretty satisfactory. Measure to be sure they will be able to carry one-quart containers of milk, fat jars of pickles and tall bottles of salad dressing. Or plan on transferring these items to smaller containers.

Does the side-by-side refrigerator offer the same (or more) practical carrying capacity as the standard over-and-under refrigerator? Would you rather have the extra freezer capacity of a side-by-side refrigerator or would you prefer the slide-out pantry that may accompany a standard over-and-under refrigerator?

Check the slideout pantry. It may look big but will it accommodate boxes of cold cereal and bags of potato chips or just small sizes of canned goods?

Be sure there is adequate cupboard space for skillets, pans, toaster, coffee pot, crock pot, bowls, dishes and all the other kitchen paraphernalia you'll be taking on the road. Will the height and depth of your cupboards accommodate the size of these items?

Linoleum or tile on the kitchen floor and under the kitchen table allows easy cleanup.

A queen-size, island bed is easy to get in and out of. If two of you will be sleeping in that bed, both of you should lie down on the bed at the same time. Will you be comfortable on that bed night after night for months at a time?

Measure the RV's mattress and see if form-fitting sheets are available. Not all RV mattresses have the same dimensions as those in your house.

Here are the standard mattress sizes according to a mattress manufacturer:

California King	72" by 84"
Eastern King	76" by 80"
Queen	60" by 80"
Full	53" by 74"
Twin	38" by 74"

There's nothing wrong with a mattress that isn't a standard size, but you do want to make an informed decision.

It doesn't make sense to hang your clothes neatly in a closet only to have the bottom six inches laying rumpled on the closet floor. Compare the interior measurements of the RV's wardrobe closet to the measurement of the garments you expect to hang in that closet.

At home, measure from the top of the clothes rod to the bottom of the longest item of clothing you expect to hang in your RV's closet. Next, measure the shoulder width of the widest clothes you will hang in your RV's closet. Finally, measure from the top of your clothes rod to the bottom of the shirts and slacks you have on hangers.

In the RV, measure the depth of the RV's closet and the distance from the top of the RV's clothes rod to the floor of the closet

Use these measurements to determine if the RV's clothes closets and shirt lockers will accommodate the clothes you wish to take.

You'll be bringing clothes for a variety of temperatures and weather conditions. Be sure there is enough closet, drawer and cupboard space for your clothes.

Most drawer items will fit one way or the other, but some RVs have more drawers with larger dimensions.

Open every drawer. You'd will be surprised at how short some of them can be. Compare the number and size of the drawers in the kitchen, bedroom and bathroom of every prospective rig. We saw one RV that had no drawers for clothes storage. The designer obviously does not wear socks or underwear.

Check out the bathroom. Is the medicine cabinet deep enough and are its shelves high enough to accommodate the items you plan to put in it?

Some folks install a short barrier on each medicine cabinet shelf to prevent the contents from spilling out after a day on the road. Is the medicine cabinet deep enough for you to do the same?

Sit on the commode. Do your knees press up to the wall or bathroom door? Is the toilet paper accessible?

Take your shoes off and step into the shower. Go through the motions of taking a shower and washing your hair. Can you accomplish this without bruising your knuckles on the ceiling or getting wrapped up in the shower curtain?

Be reasonable, most RV showers won't compare to the one you have at home, but do measure and compare the various RV showers available for the type and size rig you are looking at.

Is the bathroom vent located where it can exhaust the steam from the shower?

If the towel holders that come with the RV are insufficient or too small, you can install your own. But where? Measure the available wall or door space.

Be sure there are plenty of conveniently located electrical outlets throughout the RV.

Try everything on for size. Keep in mind that the minor inconveniences you are able to tolerate during a brief vacation can become serious aggravations on a long trip.

The best RV for extended travel, just as for vacationing or fulltiming, is the one that will take you where you want to go and let you do the things you want to do.

Slide-Out Rooms

"We're writing to you with the hope that some of your readers will assist my wife and I by providing us with information about slide-out rooms in RVs. My wife loves the extra room but I am aware of the weight differences that the slideout adds to the coach.

My biggest concerns center around the possibilities of water, air and exhaust fumes leaking into the coach. Will there be noises and rattles? How about system failures? We are looking forward to the experienced words of wisdom from readers with RV slideouts."

Joe: We published this question and asked our readers to respond. Surprisingly, we did not receive many negative comments about slideouts. Those who wrote were especially enthusiastic about the additional interior space and seemed pleased with the performance of their slideout-equipped trailers and motorhomes. They were also generous with their advice.

As part of our decidedly non-technical research, Vicki and I evaluated a 37-foot, slideout-equipped, gasoline powered motorhome. We traveled and lived in it for two weeks. We also looked closely at a number of trailers and motorhomes with a variety of slideout rooms and mechanisms.

According to those who wrote, the manufacturers have satisfactorily dealt with the problems of dust, fumes and moisture leaking into the coach. Slide-out owners emphasized, however, the importance of good seals around the slide opening. Good advice. One RV we looked at had daylight showing between the wall of the extended slide and the floor of the coach.

Look for two sets of seals. One for the extended position and the other for retracted. See if the seals "squeegee" the water from the walls and roof as the room retracts.

Owners also recommended equipping the RV with a "slide topper," an awning that keeps water, dirt and twigs from collecting on the roof of the slideout room. One owner said they added the awning after ice accumulated on their slide's roof and prevented them from retracting the room.

Be sure you test drive the unit. There shouldn't be any wind whistle, rattles or creaking while you are traveling.

We wondered if the presence of the slide-out's wall behind the driver's seat would be a distraction. I wasn't even aware of the wall being there when I drove. Two letter writers agreed.

Vicki: We spoke with owners who specifically chose RVs that were functional with the room retracted. They wanted to be sure they could stay in those few RV parks that couldn't accommodate slide-out rigs. We discovered there were times when it would have been inconvenient to extend the slide. The ability to live comfortably with the slide retracted was something we appreciated in our test unit.

We stayed in commercial RV parks while we were traveling in our slideout. There were no problems finding campsites wide enough. At first though, we had to remind ourselves to park further to the right in the campsite than we were accustomed to.

When children were around, we were more comfortable if one of us stood outside as a "spotter" while the room was extended or retracted.

A couple of owners mentioned that it took more time for the heater and air conditioners to warm up and cool down the interior. We discovered that the insulation on the walls and floors of some slide-out rooms was less than in the rest of the coach.

Several people commented on how much they like the slides that provide openable windows at each end of the slide-out room. I know we enjoyed the light airy feeling afforded by these windows.

Nobody mentioned having any difficulty with the two-inch difference between the levels of the coach and slide-out floors. The front edge of the couch and the ends of the bench-seat dinette in our borrowed motorhome were flush with the edge of the slide-out floor and presented no problems. We have seen a couple of table and chair arrangements, however, where dining room chairs perched precariously close to the floor's drop-off.

Some manufacturers have slide-out rooms whose floors drop flush with the coach floor. We have also seen a number of RVs, though, where the difference in floor levels in front of the couch bordered on being a hazard.

Most of the slide-out owners acknowledged they had sacrificed interior and exterior cabinet space but felt the extra elbow room was worth it.

We, along with others, noticed a slight decrease in fuel mileage with the slide-out units. All of us, however, were in longer rigs. It is difficult to say how much of the decrease was due to the added weight of the room and how much was attributable to the heavier weight of the bigger RV.

It seems reasonable to assume, though, that an identical RV without the slide-out room would have more cargo carrying capacity and possibly get better fuel mileage.

Pay particularly close attention to the slide's drive mechanism. If the drive system gets out of adjustment it can cause damage.

We kept track with our test vehicle. Between normal use and demonstrations for the curious, the slide-out room was extended and retracted 28 times in a two-week period. The mechanism worked flawlessly every time.

Unfortunately, mechanical things do break down. Ask the salesperson to demonstrate how the room is manually retracted if the mechanism fails to operate for some reason.

One owner, who observed the slide's hydraulic hoses passing through a storage compartment, expressed concern about the possibility of leaking hydraulic fluid.

Another wrote "I will never have another RV without a slide (even if I experience difficulties later)". And another said they are looking forward to multiple slides on their next RV.

Joe: Vicki and I are contrarians. It is not unusual for us to head south when others drive north. So don't be shocked when we tell you we prefer not to have a slide-out model. The extra aisle space just isn't important to us.

We are extended RV travelers. We generally travel two to three hundred miles a day, rarely stay in one place longer than two or three days and are on the road for two to three months at a time.

Setting up camp, for us, means parking, leveling, and connecting only those hookups we absolutely need. Getting ready to travel involves nothing more than disconnecting the hookups and starting the engine. The interior of our RV is always ready to travel.

Minimal campground setup, lots of convenient storage space and maximum cargo-carrying capacity are more important to us than extra aisle space.

We missed the deep cabinets over the couch and dinette. (By the way, we prefer a bench seat dinette because it provides storage under the seats and can double as a guest bed.) We also left a lot of "stuff" behind in our 32-foot motorhome's exterior bays that wouldn't fit in the bays of the 37-foot slideout.

Vicki didn't appreciate how much she uses the kitchen table during meal preparation until the slideout moved the table away from the kitchen counter.

Besides, like you, we have neglected to secure the refrigerator door and have had RVers wave us down to remind us we had forgotten to raise the entry step or lower the TV antenna. I don't know if I could handle someone reminding me we had forgotten to retract the slideout.

Do your homework. Compare the various makes and models. Ask owners of slideouts what they would look for in their next RV. Judging by the letters we received, there is minimal downside to a slideout and once you have experienced the added space you'll never want to do without one.

Microwave/Convection Ovens

I am accustomed to using a microwave oven, but our new motorhome will have a combination convection/microwave oven. How does this compare to the regular oven in my house?

Vicki: Once you get used to it, I think you'll find the microwave/ convection oven to be the best of all worlds. It gives you the speed of microwave cooking and the crisping and browning capabilities of a regular oven. As with anything new, it may take a little patience to become comfortable using it.

When we got our present motorhome, I was thoroughly intimidated by the convection oven. I read the instruction manual from cover to cover and started experimenting. And, just like my other cooking experiments through the years, some things turned out great, some didn't. Now that I've learned how to use my convection/microwave oven, I'm hooked. I like it so well that we bought one for our house, too.

Our RV, like so many others, came equipped with a Sharp microwave/convection oven. The one in our house, however, is made by General Electric. I've discovered that, although the specific instructions are different for each, the same basic principles apply. When giving examples, I'll refer to the Sharp model since it is the brand most commonly used in RVs.

A microwave/convection oven is like having two ovens in one. The microwave settings are used to defrost, reheat and cook just as with any other microwave oven. The convection settings are used to heat and cook similar to the way you use the oven in your house. However, because the microwave/convection oven has a high-speed fan that circulates the heat source around the food, it is hotter and, therefore, faster than a regular oven.

The "Convection" setting is best used for foods requiring a short (under 20 minutes) baking time, such as cookies, biscuits and unfilled pie crusts. Follow recipe or package instructions for temperature and cooking times; but, because the fan slightly speeds the cooking process you may find it necessary to reduce your usual cooking time by about one minute for each ten minutes baking time.

Round pizza pans are great for baking. They fit into the oven well and are great for cookies, biscuits and rolls. Place one pan on the baking rack and one on the turntable for two-level baking. You'll be able to bake twice the number of cookies, rolls or appetizers.

The "Broil" setting can be used for meats or any other food that you would broil in a conventional oven. Check the instruction booklet that came with your oven to determine the proper cooking times.

Now for the best part of a microwave/convection oven. It's called "Automatic Mix Cooking", or, "Combination Cooking". Automatic Mix cooking has two settings: "Low Mix/Bake" and "High Mix/Roast". Although each setting has been pre-programmed using a specific percentage of microwave energy and oven temperature, your oven may allow you to change the pre-programmed temperature when necessary.

Use the Low Mix/Bake setting for baked foods that require more than 20 minutes. Breads and cakes bake perfectly. Low Mix is pre-programmed to provide a combination of 10 percent microwave energy with 350 degrees oven temperature. Food cooks faster while simultaneously turning brown and crisp. Program the oven for three-quarters of the time called for in a traditional recipe or on the package. There is no need to preheat the oven when using the "Low/Mix Bake" setting.

When making packaged brownies, the instructions on the package say to bake them in a conventional oven for 50 minutes. When using the Low Mix setting on the convection oven, they only need to bake about 34 minutes.

Use the "High Mix/Roast" setting for casseroles, meat, poultry and fruit pies. This will provide a combination of 30 percent microwave energy and 300 degrees oven temperature. Meats will be juicy and moist on the inside while brown and crisp on the outside. Cooking times for foods prepared using the the High Mix setting will be reduced by roughly one-third to one-half the time required in a conventional oven, and there is no need for preheating. Just to be on the safe side, check your instruction book for the proper temperature and time.

Using the High Mix setting, I can cook a four-pound turkey breast for about 65 minutes instead of the usual 90 minutes or so in a conventional oven. The meat always turns out moist on the inside and brown and crispy on the outside. Apple pies turn out picture perfect--far superior to the ones I've made for years using regular ovens.

The convection oven, just like anything new, will take some getting used to. Start out by reading the instruction manual from cover to cover so you're familiar with the principles involved. Then, as a learning experience, prepare at least one recipe from each category (Microwave, Convection, Broil, Low Mix/Bake, High Mix/Roast) of the manual's cookbook section.

Once you familiarize yourself by using the recipes in the cookbook, you'll find it's easy to convert your own recipes. When in doubt, you can convert the baking time of each of your traditional recipes to one of the microwave/convection oven settings by referring to a similar recipe in your instruction book. Don't be afraid to experiment.

Don't let that new oven intimidate you. With a little time and some patience, you'll be cooking comfortably.

Joe: And I get to eat the experiments.

Clothes Washer/Dryers

We will be buying a larger RV within the next few months. We plan to spend long periods of time on the road. I can't decide whether or not to get a washer and dryer. Do you have one in your RV?

Vicki: Clothes washers and dryers are offered as an option in many of today's RVs. Some owners of larger RVs install apartment-size stack washers and dryers, but most RVers prefer the smaller, front-loading, combination washer/dryers. These compact machines both wash and dry the clothes.

Before you jump on the appliance bandwagon, however, there are a few things you might want to consider:

The price of a washer/dryer runs in the neighborhood of $1,000.00. Laundry room washers and dryers, on the other hand, have a larger load capacity and charge, on average, about $2.50 to do a load of clothes. Do the math. Will you use the RV washer/dryer enough to justify the expense?

A washer/dryer (33 ½ inches high, 23 ½ inches wide and 22 inches deep) fills up a good size storage cabinet. Are you willing to give up the storage space?

A washer/dryer adds about 160 pounds to one side of your rig and reduces your RV's cargo carrying capacity by that same amount. Will this compromise the RV's weight ratings?

On the other hand you could have the luxury of doing your laundry in the comfort and convenience of your RV. No lugging clothes and laundry supplies to and from the laundry room. No waiting for machines to become available. And no wondering who washed what in the Laundromat machine you are about to use.

The RV combination washer/dryer is not as big as the washer or dryer in your house. The drum of an RV washer/dryer is 1.5 cubic feet, while the drum of an average residential washer is 3 cubic feet. So that means you will only do about half the load of clothes you may be accustomed to (some RVers claim they put a set of queen-size sheets and pillow cases into a single load. Others say they only do one queen-size sheet and two pillow cases).

Depending on your choice of fabric settings, the wash cycle can take anywhere from 30 to 45 minutes; about the same as your machine at home. However, because the dryer is only 120 volts, it takes from 60 to 90 minutes to dry a load of clothes... even longer for heavy items like towels and jeans.

The washer/dryer requires 115 volts of AC electricity and draws about 13 amps while operating. A 30-amp campground hookup will provide the necessary electrical power but that leaves only 17 amps to meet the rest of the RV's needs. Operating your high amperage air conditioner, space heater or hair dryer while the washer/dryer is in use could overload a 30-amp circuit.

Ask the manufacturer of your RV if it is okay to use the washer/dryer without having full hookups (some washer drains do not go into the holding tank). The RV's generator can provide power, the fresh water tank can supply the water, and the gray water tank can capture the wash and rinse water. One load of clothes, however, consumes 16 to 20 gallons of water, and sometimes even more. That could put a serious dent in your rig's self-containment capabilities. You wouldn't want the washing machine to empty your fresh-water tank nor overflow your gray-water tank.

You have your choice of installing a vented or non-vented unit. The washing process and time is identical in both machines. The drying time, however, takes longer in the un-vented units.

Vented machines, during the drying process, take room air, heat it, tumble it through the clothes and exhaust it to the outside. This means a hole has to be made in the wall of the RV for the exhaust vent. It also means opening a window or vent so air being consumed by the dryer can be drawn into the RV.

Non-vented machines heat the existing air inside the drum and tumble it through the clothes. This creates steam within the drum. Cold water is then used to cool the outside of the drum. This condenses the steam to water which is pumped into the RV's drain and holding tank. The non-vented machine's drying process takes more time and consumes an additional 3 to 5 gallons of water.

A lot of RVers prefer to have their washer/dryer installed at the factory. The hope is that the factory's technicians might be more experienced with installing washers in their particular RV.

It's also not a bad idea to install a drain pan under the washer. The pan can protect the RV's floor by catching any spills or leaks that might occur and draining them outside.

The secret to successful clothes washing is to not overload the machine. Smaller loads not only wash and dry more completely, they come out with less wrinkles.

Here are a few suggestions that will minimize wrinkling:

Add a small amount of fabric softener to the rinse cycle. In addition to helping prevent wrinkles it will soften the clothes and make them smell fresh.

Shake out the clothes between the washing and drying cycles and occasionally during the drying process.

Remove cotton/polyester clothes from the dryer before they are completely dry. Put them on hangers in the shower to finish the drying process. Most of the time, they will end up wrinkle free.

Take the clothes out of the dryer as soon as the cycle has finished. This will prevent further wrinkling.

Don't forget to clean out the dryer lint filter after each load. And empty the washer filter every third or fourth load.

Having a washer/dryer in an RV may seem a luxury to some. To others it is a necessity. Either way, most who do have a washer/dryer seem to appreciate it as much as they do their automatic levelers, GPS or satellite TV.

Switching From Gas To Diesel

"What's it like to switch from a gasoline-powered RV to a diesel for the first time? What's the difference between operating and driving a diesel as opposed to a gas vehicle? Do you really have to understand all that techno-jargon to be a successful diesel RVer?"

Joe: We didn't know the answers to your questions. Vicki and I had never operated any kind of diesel-powered vehicle. Nobody can ever accuse us of being technical experts. Who, we asked, would be better qualified to find out?

Our evaluation unit was a 37-foot, diesel-pusher motorhome. It was powered by a Cummins 230 horsepower, 5.9 liter, turbo-charged engine. This is the diesel engine that is most often compared to the big-block gasoline-powered engines when experts discuss gas versus diesel.

Vicki: We spent three hours with a "walk through" expert employed by a local dealer who specializes in selling diesel-powered motorhomes.

When I turned the ignition key to start the engine, a buzzer screamed at me. "This motorhome is equipped with air brakes." the walk-through specialist explained. "That's the low air-pressure warning. Watch the air-pressure gauge. When it reaches 60 pounds per square inch the buzzer will stop and the transmission will allow you to go into gear."

It took a minute or so before the buzzer finally shut itself off. "Now flip that lever to fill the suspension system's air-bags" he directed. Silently and almost imperceptibly the motorhome rose a couple of inches.

The brake pedal was hinged at the floor and resembled an accelerator pedal. It took a few practice touches before I stopped throwing everyone into their seat belts. Air brakes are sensitive.

I pushed the accelerator to the floor as we entered a freeway. There wasn't a neck-snapping jolt but the motorhome moved out smartly. We merged into the freeway traffic at 55 miles per hour.

When decelerating on level roads, the diesel engine seemed to slow the motorhome almost as well as the gasoline engines in other motorhomes I had driven.

Just before reaching the freeway off ramp, I switched on the exhaust brake. When I lifted my foot from the accelerator, it felt as if I had thrown out an anchor. The engine, assisted by the transmission automatically shifting to a lower gear, really pulled the speed down. Wow!

By the time we had driven six blocks through stop and go traffic, I was touching the brakes like a pro. Air pressure remained constant in spite of the repeated use of the brake pedal.

Once the parking brake was set, I flipped the air-dump switch to deflate the suspension air bags. With a sigh the motorhome sank closer to the ground.

We learned that the engine oil, transmission fluid and coolant levels could all be checked by opening an outside compartment at the rear of the motorhome.

An air cleaner indicator was also located in this compartment. This gadget lets you know when it's time to change the air filter. A diesel engine consumes a lot of air, so it's important that the airway remains unrestricted.

Finally, we were introduced to the fuel-water separator. Here, water and sediment are separated from the fuel and settle into the bottom of a transparent bowl. A drain valve at the bottom of the bowl allows you to drain any accumulated water or sediment. The manual suggests this be done every driving day.

I made sure that Joe was paying close attention to these last few details.

Joe: We spent the months of January, February and March traveling and living in that diesel motorhome with a small car in tow. Our coast to coast route took us across mountains and desert. Temperatures ranged from 20 to 95 degrees. One year ago, we had taken the same route with identical conditions in a 36-foot gasoline-powered motorhome. It was a fair comparison of the two power plants.

Driving the diesel wasn't much different than driving a gasoline rig. Put it in gear, step on the accelerator and go. Acceleration was a little bit slower in the diesel. Hill climbing speed was about the same. Our impression was that while the gasoline-powered motorhome moved across the country satisfactorily, the diesel rig accomplished it effortlessly.

The exhaust brake took all the thrill out of driving down a long, steep hill. On one 12-mile, six-percent downgrade (with our car in tow) I only touched the airbrakes twice.

The diesel's fuel consumption was a consistent 10 miles per gallon. Last year's gasoline rig got between 6 and 7 miles per gallon.

The diesel's preventive maintenance costs are higher than the gasoline rig's. One of our local RV dealerships charges $185 to change a diesel's oil and oil filter versus $54 for a gasoline motorhome. Changing a diesel's air and fuel filters would run an additional $200 as opposed to $60 for a gasoline rig.

When we summed up the overall cost of fuel, oil and filter changes, the cost per mile was about the same for both rigs.

We learned that a diesel owner must pay particular attention to the quality of fuel that goes into the RV's tank.

Water can get into diesel fuel from the condensation that results when a fuel station's storage tanks sit partially empty for long periods of time

The presence of water in diesel fuel can corrode vital engine parts. It also permits the growth of micro-organisms in the fuel. This slimy fungus will eventually clog the fuel filter and, if not destroyed, make its way into the fuel injector pump and injectors. You don't want that to happen.

Neither do the commercial truckers. They can't afford, nor would they tolerate, getting a tank of bad fuel. It only made sense, then, to get our fuel at a reputable, busy truck stop.

We discovered a number of truck stops that had RV fuel islands. More and more truck stops are welcoming RV drivers. Check them out.

Diesel fuel is susceptible to cold weather. When temperatures drop into the low teens, the fuel begins to thicken. To help prevent this, refiners blend and winterize their fuel according to the location of the country and its expected temperatures.

We refueled every two to three hundred miles with fuel that had been blended for that area's expected temperatures.

Even though outside temperatures dropped to 20 degrees, we experienced no problems.

Going to high volume truck stops also assured us we weren't buying last summer's fuel.

Vicki: We made a couple of other observations about the difference in having a diesel RV.

Leaving a campground quickly and quietly in the pre-dawn hours was no longer an option with the diesel. If the roar of the required three minute engine warm up didn't wake up our neighbors, the scream of the air-pressure warning buzzer did.

I appreciated the fact that the rear pusher design removed the engine noise from the driver's compartment. Conversation could be held in a normal tone of voice.

That and the way the diesel chassis' air-bag suspension system seemed to float the motorhome over the highway made me a convert.

What's it like to switch from a gasoline-powered RV to a diesel for the first time? It's exciting, interesting and easy to do.

What's the difference between operating and driving a diesel as opposed to a gasoline-powered RV? Not that much, actually. The diesel just seems to do the job with less effort.

Do you really have to understand all that techno-jargon to be a successful diesel RVer? We still don't. But the diesel owner should make a point of becoming familiar with the characteristics of diesel fuel and the importance of maintaining and protecting the diesel's fuel delivery system.

Operating and maintaining a diesel engine (just like a gasoline engine) takes a bit of knowledge and thought. But after you've done it for a while it becomes second nature. Just put it in gear, step on the accelerator and go.

About Diesel Fuel

Diesel engines, because they have fewer moving parts, enjoy a reputation of having fewer mechanical problems than gasoline engines. When they do have problems, though, chances are they will be fuel related.

If you are thinking about buying a diesel-powered RV, make a point of becoming familiar with the characteristics of diesel fuel and the importance of maintaining and protecting the diesel's fuel delivery system.

A good place to begin is the ratings and grades of the over-the-road diesel fuels available.

Owners of gasoline vehicles are accustomed to seeing the octane rating of the fuel they purchase. Diesel fuel's loose counterpart is called "cetane." Cetane is a measure of the fuel's ignition quality. The higher the rating, the faster the fuel will ignite.

Fuels with a cetane rating below 40 may cause hard starting, engine knock and poor mileage. Since nearly all diesel refined in the United States has a cetane rating of at least 40, you probably won't see a selection of cetane ratings on diesel pumps.

You may, however, see two grades of diesel fuel available, 2D (Grade Number 2) and 1D (Grade Number 1).

2D is the grade most diesel engine manufacturers specify for optimum performance and the one you'll see available at most diesel pumps.

The good news about 2D diesel fuel is that its high paraffin content gives it a lot of power. The bad news is the paraffin begins to crystallize when temperatures drop into the teens.

The temperature reading when this crystallization begins to occur is known as the "cloud point." You can actually see the fuel get cloudy from the crystals.

At cloud point the paraffin wax crystals (along with ice crystals) begin to clog up the fuel filter and restrict the fuel flow. You don't want this to happen.

As the temperature continues to drop and reaches 10 degrees or less, the wax crystals thicken and prevent fuel flow altogether. The temperature reading when this occurs is referred to as the "pour point". You really don't want this to happen.

The good news about 1D diesel fuel is that its lower paraffin content means its "cloud point" and "pour point" are not reached until much lower temperatures. The bad news is that its lower paraffin content means it has less power than 2D diesel fuel.

To deal with the effects of cold weather, the refiners winterize their fuels with additives or by blending 1D fuel with 2D fuel. The fuel is winterized or blended according to the location of the country and its expected temperatures. The lower the expected temperatures, the lower the "cloud point" of the fuel shipped to that area.

During cold weather, diesel pumps may be posted with either the cloud point or the pour point of the fuel. Cloud point temperature is more important because that is when the fuel will start clogging the filter.

Cross country RV travelers should keep in mind that if they get caught in a Colorado mountain freeze with diesel fuel purchased at a New Mexico desert truck stop, they could conceivably end up with a tank full of gelatin.

One way to avoid this is to top off your fuel tank every two to three hundred miles with fuel blended for that region's expected temperature. Be sure you go to a busy fuel station. You don't want to take on a tank of last summer's fuel.

Before you put your diesel rig into storage, think about what the temperatures will be when you take it out. It only makes sense to fill the tank with the type of fuel that will start and run your engine when you take it out of storage.

One of the biggest concerns for diesel owners should be the presence of water in their fuel. Diesel engines depend upon their fuel to lubricate and cool tiny engine parts. Water that gets past the filters and into the engine displaces that fuel. Water that remains in the tank promotes rust. It also permits the formation of ice crystals in winter and bacterial growth during the summer.

The most common way that water gets into the fuel is condensation. Condensation takes place when moisture laden air condenses on the cool inner walls of a refinery's storage tanks, a fuel station's storage tanks or your own RV's fuel tank. The emptier the tank, the more surface available for condensation. The more humid the air, the more moisture available for condensation. The longer the condition exists, the more water there will be in the fuel.

Water is heavier than diesel fuel. It will settle to the bottom of the storage or fuel tank.

Where the water and diesel fuel interface, bacteria (live micro-organisms) can thrive. Left unchecked, this slimy fungus can coat the walls of your fuel tank and fuel lines, clog your filters and injectors and bring your vacation plans to a slimy halt.

If you discover signs of a buildup of micro-organisms in your fuel, a fungicide, formulated for diesel fuel can be added to the fuel tank. As the bacteria dies, it will show up in the filters, so change your filters more often if you treat your fuel with fungicide.

Preventing water related problems is easier than curing them. Get your fuel at a high volume fuel station. Storage tanks that are filled frequently present the least opportunity for condensation. The rapid turnover of fuel also helps keep water and bacteria to a minimum.

Top off the fuel tank if your rig is going to sit in an RV park or storage yard for a while. This will minimize the amount of fuel tank surface available for condensation.

Drain any accumulated water or sediment from the fuel-water separator every travel day. Most of today's diesel engines come equipped with a fuel-water separator.

Water and sediment are separated from the fuel and settle into the bottom of a transparent bowl. A drain valve at the bottom of the bowl allows you to drain any accumulated water or sediment. If your rig doesn't already have a fuel-water separator, install one.

Some rigs come equipped with a drain in the bottom of the fuel tank. If it's possible, drain the water from the bottom of the fuel tank once in a while.

Good, clean fuel is vital to a diesel's performance. You don't want to get a bad tank of fuel. Neither do the commercial truckers. Do what the truckers do; get your fuel at a reputable, high-volume truck stop.

A number of truck stops welcome RV business. Most of them identify themselves as travel plazas. Check them out.

Now that you know why, it will be easy to follow these few simple guidelines for the care and fueling of your diesel RV:

> Use fuel produced by a reputable refiner.
>
> Buy at a high volume fuel station.
>
> Drain the water separator every travel day.
>
> Inspect the filter bowl for unusual sediment, clouding or fungus.
>
> Change the filters according to the engine manufacturer's recommendations.
>
> Top off your fuel tank before putting it into storage.

Owning and operating a diesel RV is different but it isn't difficult. Pay particular attention to the quality of fuel that goes into the RV's tank and to the proper maintenance of its fuel delivery system. You'll keep your engine troubles, if any, to a minimum.

Choosing A Tow Vehicle

"How do I go about choosing a tow vehicle to pull a travel trailer? Should I choose the tow vehicle first and then find a trailer it can tow? Or should I first select the trailer and then find a tow vehicle that can pull it? How do I determine whether the tow vehicle will be able to handle the trailer?"

Joe: The first thing you should do is identify (but not purchase) the trailer that best suits your RVing interests and needs.

Next, you should locate (but not purchase) the tow vehicle that can best handle the size and weight of that trailer. Check the manufacturer's printed information to be sure the tow vehicle, its drive train and suspension are more than capable of towing the trailer you have in mind.

Finally, research to determine the best type of hitch for that trailer and tow vehicle combination.

In the best of all worlds, the tow vehicle will also satisfy your everyday transportation needs, both while you are traveling and in between RV trips while you are home. In the real world, don't be surprised if you have to make a number of compromises.

Once these objectives are met, all you have to do is figure out how to pay for them.

Vicki: Here are a few guidelines for choosing a tow vehicle:

Decide what kind of a vehicle will best suit both your personal and towing needs.

Visit the dealership selling that vehicle and obtain a copy of the manufacturer's trailering guide and towing recommendations.

The towing recommendations will be expressed in weight, so do your homework and ascertain the following:

The *tow vehicle's* Gross Vehicle Weight Rating (GVWR). That's the maximum weight, including passengers (at 150 pounds each), fuel, cargo (including the trailer's hitch weight) and the weight of the tow vehicle itself, that the tow vehicle can safely <u>carry</u> down the road.

The *trailer's* Gross Vehicle Weight Rating (GVWR). That's the maximum weight, including water and propane, optional equipment, cargo, accessories and the weight of the trailer itself, that the trailer can safely carry down the road.

The *tow vehicle's* Gross Combined Weight Rating (GCWR). That's the maximum total weight of the fully loaded tow vehicle and fully loaded trailer that the tow vehicle may safely handle.

The *tow vehicle's* Trailer Weight Rating. That's the maximum trailer weight the manufacturer has determined the tow vehicle may tow.

It's not out of line to assume you will load your tow vehicle to its GVWR and pull a trailer also loaded to its GVWR. If the combined weight of the two vehicles exceeds the tow vehicle's Gross Combined Weight Rating, you need to lighten the load or get a tow vehicle with a higher Gross Combined Weight Rating.

Here's another way of looking at it. Place the fully loaded trailer and fully loaded tow vehicle on a scale. The total weight of both vehicles should not exceed the tow vehicle's Gross Combined Weight Rating.

If the trailer's fully loaded weight exceeds the tow vehicle's Trailer Weight Rating, you need to lighten the trailer weight or get a tow vehicle with a higher Trailer Weight Rating.

Joe: Not enough can be said about the importance of staying well within the manufacturer's weight limitations (for both the trailer and tow vehicle). Personally, I'd feel better knowing my tow vehicle was rated to handle at least ten percent more weight than I was towing.

Choose and equip your tow vehicle so it is more than adequate to do the job. Most manufacturers offer an optional towing package. It costs less to order the package than to add the equipment after you take delivery.

When it comes to choosing between adequate power and fuel economy, I would take the power. I've never seen an RVer drive to the top of a long, steep grade, get out of his rig, kick the tires and curse his RV for having too much power.

Before you buy your RVing combination be sure the manufacturers of the tow vehicle, trailer and hitch all agree you have a towing combination that is made for each other.

Do your homework, pay attention to the manufacturer's written recommendations, allow some margin for safety and be sure the tow vehicle you choose will take you where you want to go and let you do the things you want to do.

Dinghy Towing

I am considering buying a Class A motorhome and towing a small car. I've seen motorhomes towing cars with all four wheels on the ground, on a dolly, and on a trailer. What are the advantages and disadvantages of each method? I asked this while camping last summer but the discussion generated more heat than light.

Motorhomes are a great way to travel and camp. Once they are set up in a campsite, however, it is often inconvenient to use them for local sightseeing trips. As a result, most motorhome owners eventually find themselves towing a transportation vehicle (dinghy).

There are a few things you should know, however, before you hitch up your commuter car to the back of your motorhome. First, you should find out if your motorhome is capable of towing your car. Next, you need to ascertain which towing method(s) are compatible with your car. Finally, you want to determine what towing method and equipment will best satisfy your RV lifestyle.

Every motorhome has limitations. Each is capable of carrying and towing just so much weight. The maximum amount of weight a motorhome may carry, including the weight of the vehicle itself, is called the gross vehicle weight rating (GVWR). The manufacturer posts the GVWR somewhere on the motorhome and makes it available in the motorhome's literature. The weight of the fully loaded motorhome should never exceed the manufacturer's GVWR.

The literature should also provide the motorhome's gross combined weight rating (GCWR). The weight of the fully loaded motorhome added to the weight of the fully loaded towed vehicle (car, trailer, etc.) should not exceed the motorhome's GCWR.

You can determine how heavy a car your motorhome can tow by subtracting the motorhome's GVWR from its GCWR. If, for example, a motorhome has a GCWR of 21,000 pounds and its GVWR is 16,000 pounds, the fully loaded towed vehicle can weigh up to 5,000 pounds before it exceeds the GCWR. An important exception is when the motorhome's manufacturer has established a lower weight figure for the towed vehicle. In that case you want to follow the lower figure.

The literature might also reveal that while the motorhome may be capable of *towing* a 5,000 pound load, it is only rated to *stop* a towed load of 1,500 pounds or less. This means the towed vehicle (trailer, car, etc.) should be equipped with its own braking system. One that will activate when the motorhome's brakes are applied.

The motorhome manufacturer should also be able to tell you the maximum amount of hitch weight the rear end of the motorhome has been designed to handle. Hitch weight is the amount of downward pressure exerted by the tongue (or tow bar) of the towed vehicle upon the hitch ball of the motorhome.

While the information provided by these ratings reveals how much weight the motorhome can safely handle, it doesn't tell you how well the motorhome will perform while towing a load. It's safe to assume, however, that the lighter the load, the easier it will be for the motorhome to move it.

Keeping the weight factor in mind, most motorhome owners tow dinghies that weigh between 2,500 and 3,000 pounds. A notable exception seems to be the sport utility vehicles that weigh up to 3,500 pounds.

There are three methods for towing a dinghy: all four of the dinghy's wheels on the ground; the dinghy's drive wheels on a dolly; and the entire dinghy on a car-carrying trailer.

Towing a dinghy with all four wheels on the ground is probably the easiest and most convenient method.

The hitching procedure is fairly easy. Aligning the coupler of the car's towbar with the motorhome's hitch ball usually involves one person directing while another drives the car. The availability of self-adjusting tow bars with telescoping arms, however, has made this a one-person operation.

Once the car is hooked up, the ignition key is turned to the accessory position. This releases the steering wheel lock and permits the car's front wheels to turn left or right while going around corners.

A disadvantage to this towing method is that you shouldn't back up when towing a car with all four wheels on the ground. The car's front wheels can cramp to the left or right and damage the car's steering and alignment mechanisms.

Storage of the towbar isn't a problem. Most of today's tow bars fold and can remain conveniently in place on the front of the car or on the motorhome's hitch receiver.

Check with the manufacturer of your car to determine if it can be towed with all four wheels on the ground. The transmissions of most vehicles, especially those equipped with front-wheel drive and/or automatic transmissions, can be damaged if the drive wheels are allowed to turn the transmission during towing.

If that is the case with your car, there are products that allow many vehicles with front-wheel drive and/or automatic transmissions to be towed with the drive wheels on the ground.

Transmission lubrication pumps are available that will lubricate the transmission while the vehicle is being towed. Axle-lock (and unlock) devices may be added to the drive wheels of some front-wheel drive vehicles allowing them to free-wheel. Drive shaft "un-couplers" can be installed on rear-wheel drive vehicles to separate the drive shaft from the transmission.

A professional hitch shop should mount a baseplate for the towbar on the front of the car and wire the car's brake and tail lights so they will operate in sync with the motorhome's lights. Detachable light bars (with brake and tail lights) can be used if you don't want to mess with the car's wiring. They're not as convenient but they'll do the job.

Check with the manufacturer to determine if the brakes of your motorhome are adequate to stop the additional weight of your towed vehicle. If not, consider installing one of the many products that will activate your car's brakes when you apply the motorhome's brakes.

Towing with all four wheels on the ground means installing special equipment on the car, but the ease of hitching and unhitching has made it the most popular towing method.

A tow dolly is a two-wheel trailer upon which the dinghy's drive wheels are secured. Towing with a dolly has a couple of advantages. The dolly can be equipped with brakes and the car does not need to have any special equipment (base plate, wiring, etc.), so any car can be towed.

The hitching procedure with a dolly, however, is a little more involved and time consuming than the "four wheels on the ground" method. First, the dolly has to be hitched to the motorhome. Next, the drive wheels of the car are driven up on the dolly. Then, the car is secured to the dolly with straps or chains. Finally, a light bar with brake and tail lights has to be mounted on the car.

Most dollies, by the way, are not designed to be backed with a car on board.

A dolly adds to the gross combined weight of the towing unit and its hitch weight has to be subtracted from the motorhome's cargo carrying capacity.

Towing with a dolly makes sense if the RVer will be towing different vehicles and/or the towing frequency does not justify the expense of installing tow-bar base plates and wiring.

A car-carrying trailer, like the dolly, offers the advantage of not having to equip the car for towing. The trailer comes equipped with its own brakes and lights. There is also the advantage of being able to back the trailer with the car on board. Most RVers take advantage of the trailer to carry additional equipment, a tool box or storage locker.

Loading and securing a car to a trailer involves a bit more work than loading onto a dolly.

Keep in mind that the trailer's tongue weight will add to the motorhome's gross vehicle weight (be sure it does not exceed the motorhome's hitch-weight rating), and the weight of the trailer will add to the gross combined weight of the towing combination.

There is also the question of what to do with the trailer when you reach your destination. Not many campsites are large enough to accommodate a motorhome, a trailer and a car.

The ease of hitching and unhitching a dinghy that is towed with all four wheels on the ground appeals to the RVer who travels frequently. Not having to equip a car for towing makes the dolly method attractive to many. Being able to carry more than just the dinghy is a big plus for using a trailer.

Whichever method you choose, all offer the benefit of having a convenient transportation vehicle available when you reach your destination.

Home Security and Maintenance

"You've mentioned that you are on the road for three to four months at a time. What do you do about the security and maintenance of your home while you are gone?"

Joe: It took a while to achieve but our house is as low maintenance as it can get. The yard is landscaped with plants, bushes and trees that require very little care. Weeding and trimming are only necessary about twice a year.

Everything is watered by a sprinkler system on an automatic timer. The sprinklers are timed to come on at about four o'clock in the morning. That way, if the sprinklers come on while it is raining, no one will notice. The sprinklers remain on timers year round and are adjusted according to the needs of the season.

The lawn is mowed weekly by a professional lawn mowing crew. We intentionally scheduled the lawn mowing to occur the day before trash pickup. The mowing crew places the bagged trimmings at the curb for the trash truck and the next day the trimmings are hauled away. The mowing crew comes every week; even when we are at home.

Selected interior and exterior lights are on timers. They go on and off as if we were there. In fact, they remain on timers 365 days of the year. The timers are adjusted periodically to coincide with normal daylight hours.

Mail is collected daily from our curbside mailbox and delivered to our daughter-in-law who then forwards it to us.

The mail collector also picks up throw-away ads, door hangers and any windblown trash whose presence would reveal our absence.

We discontinue and restart newspaper delivery so often we have the phone number on speed dial. By the way, we stop the newspaper at least two days before we leave. Just to make sure it really does stop.

Our next-door neighbors know they are welcome (and encouraged) to park their cars in our driveway while we are gone. It gives the impression that someone is home.

With the exception of people coming and going, our house maintains the same outward appearance whether we are at home or on the road. We frequently have neighbors who are surprised when they find out we were not at home for the past few months.

Vicki: I used to have a lot of inside house plants. As much as I enjoyed them, they were a bother when we went on the road. At first, we had a relative come inside the house and water them once a week. Then we farmed them out to friends and relatives who were willing to plant sit. But, considering the frequency and the length of time we were gone, both those solutions seemed a real imposition. So I gradually replaced the live plants with silk plants.

I am not going to reveal the specifics of the physical security of our home. Suffice it to say that Joe's law enforcement experience and security management background has a profound influence on the way our house is secured.

It would be difficult to break into our house and almost impossible to break in undetected. Once inside, a burglar's priorities would quickly change from thievery to escape. I suspect my husband has a bit of a mean streak in him.

Joe: Only you can determine the type and extent of security your home should have. There are a few common sense precautions that anyone can implement.

Make your house look occupied so as not to invite burglars. This can be as easy as installing a few inexpensive light timers and arranging for a reliable person to maintain the yard.

Install good locks on your gates, doors and windows. The idea is to make it easier to break into your neighbor's house than yours.

Leave a radio on just loud enough to be heard if you listen closely from outside a door or window. You'd be amazed at what a good deterrent this can be.

Put in an alarm system. It is a good idea to discuss this with your local police department first. Ask them what type of system would work best for your circumstances and their response policies. Then have the alarm system installed by a professional alarm company.

It is not enough to just have an alarm go off. What happens then? Will someone respond? Who? How long will it take for them to get to your home? Will they have your permission and the ability to enter the house? Who should they notify if there is a problem? Chances are you won't be able to return home for a couple of days. Who will be responsible for securing your home until you return? Put together a response plan.

Test and adjust your alarm system to be sure it only activates when it should. False alarms can result in police department fines, discontinued response and your neighbors hoping that you really do get robbed.

Minimize the losses that can occur if someone does burglarize your home. Put your cash and jewelry in a safe deposit box. Hide or secure guns and other easily pawned objects. Make it time consuming and difficult for an intruder to locate and remove your valuables.

Vicki: Our sons and daughters-in-law live nearby. They check our house periodically. A quick walk through reveals anything unusual. One of our sons also checks to make sure the alarm system, lights, sprinklers and timers are all working properly.

The neighbors know both our sons and their wives. They have their phone numbers. The neighbors have been asked to call our sons if they see anything unusual around our house.

Both of our sons are authorized to write checks on one of our checking accounts. This gives them the ability to pay for any emergency repairs that may be necessary.

As you can see, most of our home security and maintenance arrangements remain the same whether we are at home or on the road. When it's time to leave, we notify our sons, mail collector, newspaper and immediate neighbors. A few additional security precautions are put in place and off we go.

Now, if you live in a secured condominium complex, you might have very different considerations; like, how do you keep the pipes from freezing or ...

Banking and Bill Paying

"We're planning to take a series of three and four month trips beginning next summer. What preparations would you suggest we make for banking and paying our bills while we are away from home?"

Vicki: Start now, it takes time to identify the things you need to change and it takes time to implement those changes.

RVers who plan to spend more than a few weeks on the road usually have to find a way to deal with their banking and bill-paying responsibilities while they are away from home.

One method is to estimate and prepay the bills that will come due while you are absent. But, that can take cash out of interest earning accounts sooner than necessary.

Another approach is to have all your statements and bills forwarded to you by mail, then pay them as you do at home. But, chances are you will not receive your forwarded mail until at least a week after it has been delivered to your home. That means income will be deposited later than necessary and some bills could get paid late.

An easier alternative is to develop a simplified banking and bill paying system that will take care of your financial obligations not only while you are at home, but while you are on the road as well.

Ideally, such a system will minimize your need to go to the bank, minimize the amount of cash you need to carry, minimize the number of checks you have to write, and minimize the number of statements and bills you receive in the mail

You can begin to simplify your banking needs by consolidating as many of your financial affairs as possible at one financial institution. This will reduce the number of statements you receive in the mail.

Check out the services offered by banks, savings and loans, credit unions and even the brokerage houses. You probably won't need a personal relationship with your banker, so choose a financial institution that offers:

Interest-earning checking account. Many financial institutions offer a free checking account when a minimum amount of money is maintained in either the checking account or some type of savings account. The alternative seems to be a checking account that charges you a fee for the privilege of the bank using your money.

Overdraft protection. This allows you to write a check for more money (within limits) than you have in your checking account. The financial institution automatically advances or loans you the amount necessary to cover the difference. Overdraft protection provides a temporary fix in case a bookkeeping error results in you writing a check that exceeds your balance. It can also be the source of an emergency loan.

ATM card. Get an ATM card that is associated with a large network such as Cirrus, Plus or Star. An ATM card allows you to get cash just about everywhere you travel. No need to carry large amounts of cash on your person or in your RV. And, you will not have any need for traveler's checks either.

Visa or MasterCard. These credit cards are universally accepted by just about every type of merchant.

Having one (or both) of these cards allows you to eliminate all those individual merchant credit cards that clutter up your wallet and fill your mailbox with monthly statements.

Debit card. A debit card is utilized just like a credit card except that the amount of the transaction is immediately deducted from your checking (or savings) account.

Electronic deposit of income. You can arrange to have most regular sources of income such as pay checks, retirement checks or social security checks, electronically deposited to your checking or savings account.

If, for example, a check is due on the first of the month, it is electronically deposited to your account on the first of the month. No waiting for the checks to arrive, no filling out deposit slips, no going to the bank.

Electronic payment of bills. You can also arrange to have your regular monthly bills, such as mortgage payments, car payments and utility bills automatically and electronically paid each month. The money is withdrawn from your checking or savings account. When the statement arrives in the mail it will say something like "Statement Only, Do Not Pay." No waiting for the bill to arrive, no writing and mailing checks, no late charges.

Telephone banking services. By dialing an 800 number from anywhere in the country you can determine the latest deposits, withdrawals and balances of your various accounts. You can move money from one account to the other. Funds can be kept in interest bearing accounts until they are needed in your checking account.

Internet banking services. Go on the internet, bring up your financial institution's web site, enter your access code and you can see (and print out) the history and status of your accounts. No need to wait for your monthly statement to get forwarded to you in the mail. You can also instruct the financial institution's computer to move money from one account to another. You will find that internet access is available in most of today's RV parks and campgrounds.

Bank by mail   Most financial institutions will provide you with deposit slips and envelopes so you can deposit checks by mail.

Safe-deposit box   Get a large enough safe-deposit box so you can safely store any small valuables you do not want to leave at home when you travel.

Joe: Here is a suggestion of how you can use these services to develop a simple, yet consistent, banking and bill paying system:

Minimize your need to go to the bank by: banking by telephone; banking by internet; and banking by mail. Arrange to have your income electronically deposited. Electronic deposit eliminates the concern about checks lost in the mail, checks being forwarded in the mail and deposits not getting to the bank on time.

Minimize the number and expense of writing and mailing checks by automatically and electronically paying as many bills as possible (loans, utilities, etc.). Electronic payment assures you that, whether you are at home or on the road, your bills will be paid on time.

Minimize the amount of cash you need to carry by: writing checks; using your credit card; or using your debit card instead of paying cash.

When you are traveling, use your debit or credit card for as many financial transactions as possible. Purchase fuel, pay for campgrounds and buy groceries using your credit card. By the way, when you pay for groceries with a debit card, most stores will allow you to obtain cash as well. This can eliminate visits to ATMs and paying ATM fees.

Instead of waiting for your credit-card statement to be forwarded while you are on the road, go on line with your credit card company or call the Customer Service 800 number on the back of your credit card. Find out your balance or minimum payment and send them a check. If the credit card is with your financial institution, you can make payment by using the 800 number or online banking system.

Another option to waiting for your monthly credit card statement to be forwarded, is to add up the credit card receipts you have generated and write a check for the amount due.

You can also arrange to have your credit card payment automatically and electronically deducted from your bank account.

Minimize your ATM visits (and fees) by obtaining at least a week's worth of cash whenever you make an ATM withdrawal.

Minimize the number of statements and bills you receive in the mail and the number of checks you have to write by using only one financial institution and one credit card. Pay the credit card balance before interest charges are levied.

It may take a little thought and planning, but you should be able to develop a simplified, yet consistent banking and bill paying system that will take care of your financial obligations not only while you are at home, but while you are on the road as well.

Receiving Mail

"How do I arrange to have mail forwarded to me when I am on the road?"

Joe: RV travelers can easily arrange to have their mail forwarded to them while they are on the road.

The first and most important step is to find a reliable person who is willing to retrieve your mail from your home mail box, put it into an envelope and then send it to you on the road.

Ideally, the person who is looking after your house will also be willing to forward your mail. Tell them you will call periodically to let them know where it should be sent.

When you are ready to receive your mail, look at a map and identify a town that you will be staying near, or traveling through, in about five days. Ask your mail forwarder to put all your mail into a single envelope and address it as follows:

Your Name
c/o General Delivery
City or Town, State, Zip Code

The receiving post office will hold your mail for up to thirty days before returning it to the sender. Retrieving your mail is simply a matter of going to the post office and showing the postal clerk your personal identification.

Here are a few tips to make things work smoothly. Select a small town to receive your mail. You, the tourist, will have an easier time locating the post office (anyone on the street will be able to give you directions). Locating a parking space near the post office for your RV will be easier in a small town. And, our experience is that small town post offices seem to keep better track of general delivery mail.

Get a *Zip Code Directory* from the post office or a book store. Not only will it provide you with each town's zip code, you will be able to tell how small a town it is. The fewer zip codes listed for a town, the fewer post office branches it has.

Not all post office branches will receive and hold general delivery mail. Once you have decided where you would like to receive your mail, call the post office at 1-800-ASK-USPS (1-800-275-8777). They will tell you which post office branch in that town can receive general delivery mail. They will also provide you with that post office branch's zip code, street address and, in some cases, directions on how to get there.

Vicki: Have your mail forwarder send your mail in a US Post Office's Priority Mail Flat Rate envelope. The post office says Priority Mail will arrive at its destination within the United States in two to three days. It usually does, but we have waited as long as five days on a couple of occasions.

Be sure to use the Priority Mail envelopes that have the words "Flat Rate" on them. Mail shipped in the regular Priority Mail envelopes are charged postage by zone and weight. Mail shipped in "Flat Rate" envelopes travel anywhere in the United States for the one-pound rate regardless of weight and distance.

Make life easy by providing your mail forwarder with a supply of the Priority Mail Flat Rate envelopes and sufficient stamps or money for postage. Priority Mail Flat Rate envelopes are free and available at most post offices. Prepaid (stamped) Priority Mail Flat Rate envelopes can be ordered online at www.usps.com for the price of the postage.

Your mail forwarder can stuff the Priority Mail Flat Rate envelope with as much mail as it will hold and send it to any town in the United States for the one-pound postage rate. Remind your mail forwarder, however, that security regulations require that any envelope weighing more than one pound must be personally handed to a postal employee.

By the way, for a small fee your mail forwarder can have the post office add a tracking number to the envelope they are sending you. If the envelope goes astray, the tracking number will make it easier for the post office to locate it.

It might be possible to limit the size and weight of the mail that is forwarded to you by specifying what pieces of mail you want forwarded. Obviously this would depend upon your circumstances and your mail forwarder.

At one time, our daughter-in-law forwarded our mail. She separated our mail into three piles. One pile was the mail we definitely wanted forwarded; first-class envelopes and other important mail (she had permission to open the envelopes if she wasn't sure). The second pile was the obvious junk mail; grocery ads, dated materials and such that she threw into the trash. The third pile was the mail we wanted her to save until we returned. That included magazines, catalogs and other items that we did not have to see right away.

Today, all our mail goes to a post office box in our home town. When we are on the road a mail servicing company retrieves our mail from the post office box and forwards it to us. They won't hold any of our mail until we return and they don't throw anything into the trash. Obviously our forwarded packages of mail are much bulkier now than when our daughter-in-law was our mail forwarding person.

It might be possible to receive your mail at a campground or RV park where you are staying. Before you make arrangements, however, ask the campground if they have a procedure in place for handling their guest's mail. Obviously, if they don't have a procedure, or if their procedure doesn't inspire confidence, you will want to make other arrangements to receive your mail. It is a good idea to have your mail forwarder make a note of your arrival date on the lower left corner of the envelope, just in case the envelope arrives at the RV park before you do.

Medical Care And Prescriptions

"What if I need medical attention while traveling? What do I do about getting my prescriptions filled?"

Joe: RV travelers should be happy to learn that good medical care and prescription refills are available just about everywhere they go. A little planning and research makes them easy to obtain.

Start out by anticipating and preparing for any potential medical problems that may be encountered during your trip.

Talk to your health insurer or HMO. Find out what procedures you should follow to obtain emergency and routine medical care while you are away from home. In most cases, you will be covered if you follow their guidelines.

If you wear prescription glasses, take a spare pair with you. And, it doesn't hurt to take a copy of the prescription, just in case. That way, if you need to get another pair along the way, you can take your existing prescription into one of the quick eyeglass centers to get new glasses instead of having to make an appointment with an optometrist for an eye examination.

If you are under the regular care of a physician, make an appointment with your doctor before leaving on an extended journey. Tell him about the trip you'll be taking. Make sure there is no medical reason to postpone it. If your doctor feels that you should visit another doctor along the way, ask for a referral.

Ask your doctor to write a summary of your medical condition for other doctors to read in case you require medical attention while traveling. You could also ask him if your medical condition would make it advisable to take a copy of your medical records with you. If so, allow plenty of time for the copying to be done. Keep in mind that, although it is possible to fax your medical records across the country, you may find yourself in a situation where you need a copy of your records on Friday night and your doctor's office doesn't open until the following Monday morning.

Vicki: If necessary, ask the doctor to prescribe a sufficient quantity of medication to last the duration of your trip. It may be possible for the doctor to prescribe a one-to-three month supply of medicine and authorize two or three refills on that same prescription.

The most important thing to be aware of when you have prescriptions to fill is that, in most cases, a prescription is good only in the state in which it is written. Do not count on being able to take a prescription written by a doctor in your home state into a pharmacy in another state to have it filled.

If you are taking a non-narcotic medication, ask your hometown pharmacist to give you your prescription and one or two of the authorized refills in a sufficient quantity to last your entire trip. Store the medicine in a cool, dark place in your RV and it should travel with no problem.

If your pharmacy or insurance company does not allow a several-month quantity to be filled at one time, or if you are taking a narcotic medication that, by law, cannot be dispensed in large quantities, you'll need to explore some other options.

Perhaps you can get your original prescription filled at your hometown pharmacy. Then, when you are ready for a refill, you could ask a relative, friend or neighbor to get the prescription refilled for you. Maybe the person who is forwarding your mail can enclose your refill in your next envelope of mail.

Check into the mail order pharmacies. You will find them advertised on the internet and in travel and RV magazines. You send a completed form along with your prescription and payment to the mail order pharmacy; they then mail the medication to you. When you are comparing mail order companies, ask for a list of the states they can and cannot mail prescriptions to. They may not be able to mail to every state.

Many extended RV travelers use nation-wide, chain pharmacies such as those at Wal-Mart and K-Mart. They get their original prescription filled at their hometown Wal-Mart. When it's time for a refill, they go into another Wal-Mart with the number on their prescription bottle. The pharmacist feeds the number into the computer and the refill order is processed.

Before relying on a chain pharmacy to get medication while on the road, it is always a good idea to check with the one in your hometown. There may be laws affecting their ability to transfer prescriptions from one store or state to another.

There are times when you may require medical treatment while traveling. If you have a medical emergency, don't hesitate. Go to an emergency hospital. Look for a big blue sign with a white "H". You'll see them along the interstates, highways and even in downtown areas. When you see that sign, you'll know that an emergency medical facility is at the next off ramp or right down the road. If you don't see a hospital nearby, ask a policeman, fireman or anyone else in the area where the nearest emergency medical facility is located. Rather than just giving you directions, they may lead you there.

If your medical problem is not a real emergency, try to avoid going to an emergency hospital. You'll have to wait while they take care of the genuine emergencies, and they will probably charge you more than a doctor's office would for the same treatment.

If you need the services of a doctor or a dentist and it's not an emergency, ask someone who works or lives in the area for a recommendation. If you are staying in a campground, don't overlook the obvious--ask someone at the campground office. They will very likely give you the name and phone number of their own doctor. You will be getting a first-hand recommendation.

You could also drive around the area surrounding a hospital. You'll usually find medical offices located in the neighborhood. If the doctor's receptionist tells you the doctor is not taking any new patients, tell her you are a traveler and do not want to become a regular patient. It might also help if you offer to pay by cash or credit card rather than through your medical insurance company.

Many RV travelers report having excellent results with the emergency, walk-in medical clinics. These clinics are located in even the smallest towns and are usually easy to find. Some of them advertise on the campground maps that you are given when you register. And, of course, you will find them in the telephone book "Yellow Pages" listed under "Medical". Many of these relatively small clinics are surprisingly well equipped and amazingly efficient. They usually have their own x-ray facilities and labs and are staffed with conscientious doctors, nurses and clerical personnel.

If one of your traveling party is ever hospitalized, ask the hospital if you can park your RV in the hospital parking lot. A number of RVers report that not only were they allowed to stay in their RVs in the parking lot, but in many cases they were even directed to a secure site where they could hook up to electricity.

Medical care and medicine are available just about everywhere you go. A little planning and preparation on your part will just make them easier to obtain.

Telephone Communications

"How do RVers keep in touch with their families while they are traveling? Should we carry a cellular telephone?"

Joe: Telephone communication while traveling is easily accomplished thanks to a variety of modern-day services and equipment.

Cellular telephones allow you to place or receive telephone calls in nearly all populated areas and along most major highways throughout the USA and Canada.

RV travelers with cellular phones feel secure knowing they can call for help in an emergency. They also have peace of mind knowing their families can reach them if there is an emergency at home.

Cellular service charges, however, can mount up quickly when you are traveling. In addition to a monthly service fee, be prepared to pay for each minute of phone usage (airtime) for both incoming and outgoing calls.

When you leave your "home" cellular company's area and travel into the geographical area of another cellular company, you become a "roamer". Generally, a "roamer's" fee is charged once on any day a cellular call is placed or received. Additionally, a "roamer" might be charged for airtime.

"Roamers" can also expect to pay long-distance charges whenever they place or receive a long-distance call. When callers dial your cellular phone number they are charged only for the standard telephone call to your "home" cellular area. You are charged for the long-distance call from your "home" cellular area to your present location.

You can control your cellular costs by limiting the number of cellular calls (both incoming and outgoing) and the amount of time spent on the cellular phone.

A lot of RV travelers use the "flat-rate" plans offered by many cellular services. They pay a flat monthly fee for a given number of airtime minutes and there are not any roaming or long-distance charges. Some "flat-rate plans also include "free" cellular minutes after 9:00 pm and on weekends and holidays.

Vicki: Telephone hookups at individual campsites are available at some RV parks. Typically, the local telephone company activates the connection and assigns you a telephone number. This service, obviously, is designed for those who intend to remain at the RV park for a period of time.

A growing number of RV parks, however, (especially the newer ones) are beginning to offer telephone hookups at their sites on a daily basis. A telephone hookup means you can place and receive calls and use your computer to go on line. You simply request and pay for the telephone hookup just as you would an electric, water or cable connection.

Pay phones can be found everywhere you go. Cellular service is not always available so chances are some of your on-the-road telephone calls will be made from pay phones.

Always make sure you access your own long-distance carrier before placing a telephone call. That way you will avoid the outrageous fees some telephone-booth owners charge unsuspecting customers.

Telephone calling cards are a convenient way to place long-distance calls. You can get one from the larger RV clubs, your local telephone service provider or from a long-distance carrier such as AT&T, MCI or Sprint. While there won't be a monthly service fee, some telephone calling cards add a surcharge for each call you place. Shop around.

By the way, don't let anyone see or hear you using your calling card number. If they are able to copy it, they can place calls that will show up on your bill.

Prepaid phone cards are another way to save money on long-distance calls. You'll find them for sale in department stores, supermarkets and drug stores.

When you purchase a prepaid phone card, you buy a given amount of telephone calling time, usually expressed in units or minutes.

You can make your calls any time, any day, and to any place in the continental United States with a prepaid phone card and the cost per minute is the same. This can be an economical advantage if you want to place long-distance calls during the daytime hours.

Do some comparison shopping. We've seen the cost vary from a high of forty cents per minute on one store's card to a low of three and one-half cents per minute on a discount store's card. Obviously, you want the card with the lowest cost per minute.

Be sure you buy from a reputable source and check to see if the card has an expiration date. You don't want to buy a card you can't use.

Joe: **Telephone answering machines** allow people to leave messages for you when they call your home telephone. You can retrieve and respond to those messages while you are on the road.

Invest in a quality telephone answering machine. Get one with a "remote retrieval" feature. This will allow you to call home while you are on the road and instruct your answering machine to relay your messages to you.

Another answering machine feature, one that will save you money, is called "tollsaver." By flicking a switch on the answering machine you instruct it to answer your phone on the first ring if anyone has left a message for you, but to wait until the fourth ring if there are not any messages.

When you call home for messages and your phone rings more than two times, you can assume there are no messages on the answering machine. You can save the cost of a toll call by hanging up before the answering machine answers the phone on the fourth ring.

When you return home, a flick of a switch instructs your machine to return to its normal answering mode.

By the way, don't invite any burglars by announcing on your answering machine that you are away from home.

Voice mail service may be offered by your local telephone company. This service is similar to an answering machine except the equipment is owned and operated by the telephone company. The phone company doesn't offer any kind of "toll saver" feature in conjunction with its voice-mail service

Commercial voice mail services advertise in RV magazines. RV clubs that offer mail forwarding usually offer some form of message service for a moderate fee.

Emergency telephone message service is offered to the members of some RV and automobile travel clubs as a benefit of membership. Typically, the caller dials an 800

number to leave an emergency message and the member dials an 800 number to retrieve the message. A service like this can be worth the price of a club's annual membership.

Pagers can reach you anywhere, anytime. The caller dials your pager number, waits for a tone, then enters the number they want you to call. Your pager beeps and displays your caller's number. Some paging systems can relay entire messages and even e-mail.

Visit a telecommunication store for more details. Be sure they understand you will be traveling out of your local area. It makes a difference in the type and cost of service.

Keep in mind that while the pager can reach you, you still have to locate a telephone in order to reply.

Some RV travelers have their callers reach them by pager. They can then decide whether to reply by using their cellular phone or the next convenient pay phone. This method allows RV travelers to control their cellular phone costs.

Most RV travelers have found that the telephone calling card, answering machine, and a cellular phone are more than adequate for their telephone needs.

Second Cellphone Solution

Joe: Cellular phones can be an RVers best friend. They give you peace of mind knowing that in an emergency, whether it's a mechanical emergency or a medical emergency, you can immediately call out and arrange for the appropriate response. Cellular phones also give peace of mind to those of us with elderly parents, children and grandchildren. We know that if there is an emergency at home we can hear about it now, not late tonight when we call home for messages. And then, there is the convenience of being able to call ahead to make sure a campground has a vacancy. Or the pleasure of being able to sit in the comfort of our RV and listen as a grandchild describes her day. Every RV traveler should carry a cellular phone.

But having a cellular phone also creates a problem. When one of us leaves the RV (to go to the store, for example), and the other is staying in the RV, who should retain possession of the cellphone? Obviously, that should depend upon who is most likely to have the greatest need for a cellphone.

That could be the person leaving the RV. For example, the husband is driving into town to go to the store. He takes the cellphone. That gives him the ability to call for assistance in case of a mechanical breakdown. His wife should be able to call him by using the campground's pay phone. They could even make arrangements for her to call him at pre-determined intervals if he is going to be absent for any length of time. If the husband carries the campground's office phone number with him and verifies that the office personnel are willing to deliver an emergency message, he can always reach his wife in an emergency by calling the campground office.

On the other hand, circumstances could dictate that the cellphone remain with the wife in the RV. When, for example, a campground office staff and/or pay phone are not available. Leaving the cellphone in the RV gives her the ability to call out in an emergency. In this case, the husband might be able to find a pay phone to periodically keep in touch with his wife in the RV.

An obvious solution is for each of them to have their own cellphone. We thought about that. But, based upon our cellphone usage, we couldn't justify the expense of an additional cellphone and service. So, after some research, we decided to add a pre-paid cellular phone to our communication gear.

Pre-paid cellular telephone service is identical to that of regular cellular phone service. The difference is that instead of contracting for service and paying a monthly service fee, you pre-pay (or buy) a given number of cellular airtime minutes; just as you do with a pre-paid phone card. The airtime minutes can be purchased in $10.00, $25.00, $50.00 and $100.00 increments. The more minutes purchased at a time, the less each minute costs.

Vicki: Pre-paid cellular phones can be found wherever regular cellphones are sold. We've even seen them at Wal-Mart. Pre-paid cellphone calls are relatively expensive (65 to 85 cents a minute) but the good news is that you do have a cellular phone available for emergencies. And if it's an emergency, you don't care that the call is costing you eighty-five cents a minute.

We decided to purchase a new cellular phone for our primary use and convert the old cellphone to a pre-paid cellular phone. The salesperson at the telephone store transferred our ATT cellular service and phone number to the new cellular phone. Then he activated the old cellphone as a pre-paid cellular phone. The pre-paid cellphone was assigned a phone number just like any other cellphone. When we place a call, we are told how many minutes of calling time remain in our pre-paid time bank. We can add minutes to our pre-paid time bank by purchasing pre-paid cellular phone cards or by making a phone call and charging the minutes to our credit card.

According to our agreement the calling time we add to the pre-paid time bank must be used within 90 days or it expires. However, if we add additional time before the 90 days is up, the old, unused minutes are carried forward for the next 90 days. We add $10.00 of minutes to our calling-time bank every 89 days. That works out to about $3.50 a month for the availability of cellular service. It also gives us about 100 minutes of calling time a year.

We usually leave the primary cellphone with the person in the RV and the pre-paid cellphone goes with the person who leaves the RV.

Our adult children are the only ones who know our pre-paid cellphone's number, and they will only call it in an emergency.

AT&T makes it real easy to purchase additional calling time, and having the pre-paid cellphone available makes it very tempting to use it. But, so far, we have kept to our plan of using it only for emergencies and an occasional brief call. Of course, we remember when our first cellular phone was purchased "for emergencies only", and then we began using it for brief calls, and then ....

Computers and RVs

"Can I take my computer in my RV? Does anyone make computer furniture for RVs? Do I need to be aware of anything special?

Joe: Yes, you can take your computer in your RV. Yes, computer desks are available for RVs. And yes, there are a few simple considerations.

The first consideration is where you are going to put the computer and all its peripheral equipment. Chances are you'll also be lugging along a printer, connecting cables, disks and manuals.

A built-in computer desk seems to make sense. That way you have a place for everything and everything can stay in its place.

A number of RV manufacturers offer built-in computer desks as an option in some of their models. If you are shopping for a new rig, ask the dealer if one is available for the RV you are considering.

Most of the RV computer desks we have seen were created by the RV owner. All of these custom desks involved removing or altering some of the RV's original furnishings. Some simply amounted to the installation of a small desk purchased at a furniture store. Others were constructed by bridging a couple of two-drawer file cabinets with some kind of a writing surface. The clever desks were those that served more than one purpose.

In most cases, a bungee cord or adjustable strap secured the computer and printer to the desk top during travel. A thick felt pad or piece of foam under the equipment dampened road vibration.

Most computer-toting RVers set up their monitors, computers and printers on an existing flat surface such as the dashboard, an auxiliary table, or even the kitchen table. Obviously, a place has to be found to secure these items when they are not being used, especially while traveling.

A popular solution for those who are unable or unwilling to make room inside their closets or cupboards is to seatbelt their computer equipment onto couches and chairs while traveling.

Vicki: Both desktop and laptop computers seem to do well in RVs. If you are contemplating the purchase of a computer for use in an RV, however, we would suggest you seriously consider the advantages of a laptop.

A laptop computer is designed to withstand some of the jolts and bumps of being carried and moved from place to place. It takes up considerably less room than a desktop and, as its name implies, it doesn't require a dedicated workspace.

We gave a lot of thought to working on the road when we purchased our most recent computer. We wanted something that would travel well, take up a minimum of space and could be easily carried between our house and the RV. While the idea of a computer desk appealed to us, we were reluctant to sacrifice the furniture and space it would take.

We purchased a laptop computer and a notebook size printer. Computer, printer, cords and cables all fit into a briefcase. A versatile folding table, 16 inches by 32 inches, provides additional desktop area when needed. The table stores flush against the end wall inside our wardrobe closet when not in use.

We especially appreciate the versatility and portability of the laptop. It has the ability to operate on a variety of power sources; regular electricity, plugged into a cigar lighter or using its own built-in battery. That means we can use it at the kitchen table, in the passenger seat, or while sitting in a lawn chair.

I frequently work with our laptop sitting in my lap as we drive on interstates (and you know how smooth they are). I haven't experienced any problems.

During a trip to Alaska, one of our caravan members, a writer, worked on her desktop computer while her husband drove. To my knowledge, they never encountered any computer problems either.

Be careful, though, if you plan to use your computer while traveling. We have been told that a good jolt could bring the hard-drive's read/write head into contact with the hard-drive and cause it to crash. This is one more reason to back up your computer's hard drive.

By the way, generator and campground power is subject to surges, spikes and other aggravations. Be sure to use a surge protector when operating your computer and printer.

E-Mail and Internet Connections

"Will I be able to connect to the internet and receive e-mail while I am traveling in my RV?"

Joe: There are a number of ways for RV travelers to connect to the internet and do their e-mail. The one you choose will depend upon your interests, needs and budget.

Dial-up Connection. Essentially, you plug your computer into an available telephone jack and dial your internet service provider. This method is relatively inexpensive and requires no additional equipment,

To do this, you might want to sign up with an internet service provider (ISP) that provides a list of local telephone-access numbers in cities and towns around the country. This will allow you to program your computer to dial a local (and, therefore, toll-free) telephone number to connect to your ISP. Ideally, your ISP will also provide an 800 number to use when a local number is not available.

The simplest way to have a dial-up connection is to stay at an RV park or resort that provides telephone hookups at each campsite. Unfortunately, telephone hookups are not a commonplace amenity at most campgrounds. However, an increasing number of RV parks and campgrounds, while unable to justify the expense of retrofitting all their sites with telephone hookups, are installing telephone jacks in their offices, lounges, or laundry rooms so their guests can plug in their laptop computers and go online.

Bear in mind, though, that the telephone jacks located in campground offices are intended for brief usage only. The idea is to go online, send your prepared e-mail, download your incoming e-mail and get off the line. These connections are not intended for the folks who want to surf the net, go into chat rooms or research their family's genealogy.

If you need to spend more time online here are a few suggestions:

The campground telephone jacks are usually less busy before 4:00 pm and after 10:00 pm. You may be able to spend some time online during the non-busy hours without inconveniencing other campers.

And, there are other places where you can do your e-mail on the road. RVers have discovered that many of the large truck stops, like the Flying J Travel Plazas, have telephone jacks available at their payphones. Some even have sit-down booths with a telephone jack for laptop users. Ask the person at the fuel desk or the cashier at the travel plaza's restaurant if they have facilities for you to plug in your laptop.

Kinkos fast-print shops are nationwide and many are open 24-hours a day, seven days a week. They advertise PC and Mac rental stations. For a nominal fee you can access the internet using their computers. If you have your own laptop they may not charge you for the use of their rental stations.

Many public libraries have computers available for the public to access the internet, usually at no charge. You may have to reserve a block of time at some of the busier libraries, though.

Obviously, the downside to the dial-up connection may mean lugging your laptop to the telephone jack's location and perhaps waiting for your turn to go online.

Cellular Connection. Many RVers connect their computer to their cellular phone with a cable obtained from their cellular service provider. The cellular phone provides the telephone connection with their internet service provider. Depending upon their cellular service provider, the RVer dials a local access or a toll-free telephone number, or perhaps clicks an icon on their computer screen to gain access to the internet.

While more convenient than using the dial-up connection at the campground office, cellular connectivity is dependent upon a reasonably strong and uninterrupted cellular signal. Something that is not always available in remote areas. And, transmitting data via a cellular telephone can be agonizingly slow. As a result, most RVers have a tendency to limit their cellular connection to sending and receiving e-mail.

Wireless Modem Card. Some cellular service providers also offer a PCMCIA wireless modem card with an antenna. It provides a cellular connection without having to connect to a cellular telephone. It is often referred to as an aircard. The connection is usually at a higher speed than that of the cellphone. Usage however requires a service contract that some consider a bit pricey.

Wi-Fi Connection. Wi-Fi, short for wireless fidelity, is a technology that allows a Wi-Fi enabled desktop or laptop computer to connect to the internet via radio signals. The connection takes place in the vicinity of a wireless-access point called a "hotspot".

A hotspot is a location (campground, travel plaza, restaurant, etc.) that is hard-wired into the internet and has installed a Wi-Fi radio that can simultaneously "talk" to a number of Wi-Fi enabled computers. The computers need only be within range of the hotspot's radio antenna(s) in order to have a high-speed wireless connection to the internet.

Some hotspots permit the computer user to go online free. Others may ask for a credit card number and charge an hourly, daily, or monthly usage fee.

Many new computers already come with a built-in Wi-Fi card. It is an easy matter, though, to add a Wi-Fi card to older laptop or desktop computers. Laptop owners need only purchase a special PCMCIA card that is inserted into their laptop's PCMCIA slot. Desktop owners can either buy and install a Wi-Fi card, or purchase an adapter that connects to the computer with a USB cable. Once a computer is equipped with a Wi-Fi card it can access the internet through any available hotspot in the country.

Obviously, the advantage of Wi-Fi is the ability to go online from the comfort and convenience of your RV. The connection is usually fast and reliable. The downside could be in locating a hotspot and the cost of using it.

Satellite Connection. Some RVers are connecting to the internet using a two-way satellite internet dish. The dish can be permanently mounted on the roof of the RV. It may even be able to search out and lock onto the appropriate satellite. Satellite internet service is available anywhere the dish has a clear view of the southern sky. This makes it ideal for the RVer who frequents remote areas and wants a high-speed internet connection.

The equipment, installation and monthly service fee for satellite internet service, however, is quite a bit more expensive than the other options.

Vicki: Connecting to the internet and doing your e-mail, while still an occasional adventure, is no longer a challenge.

Dial-up connection, while the least expensive, may also be the least convenient. But it will do the job. And when the other methods fail, dial-up is usually the back-up connection.

Cellular connection involves the relatively low purchase price of the connecting cable and, depending upon your cellular service plan, the cost of the airtime minutes used. It is convenient but it can be slow and requires a reliable cellular signal.

Wi-Fi is both fast and convenient. The initial investment in a PCMCIA card is relatively low and there are free hotspots available. But, hotspots are not everywhere and some do charge a usage fee.

Satellite internet service is also fast and convenient. But the initial investment is expensive and the monthly service fee is relatively high when compared to the other internet connection methods.

Office On The Road

Joe: Our RV seminar business is conducted nationwide. Like most businesses, it is heavily dependent upon communication. Unlike most other businesses, though, we operate from a traveling motorhome for two to four months, switch to our stationary home office for two or three months, and then move back into the RV again.

Setting up a portable office and communication system that would function consistently whether we were in the motorhome or our home office was a challenge. We determined to keep it simple, functional and inexpensive.

The home office was set up first. We have two telephone lines. The primary line is for incoming business calls. The secondary line is used to place outgoing calls. The secondary line is also shared by our computer and the fax machine. Vicki and I spend very little time on the internet during business hours, and faxes rarely happen anymore, so sharing the outgoing telephone line with the equipment is not a problem.

A cellular telephone is an absolute necessity if you are going to conduct business on the road. Shop around to find the cellular provider and service plan that best suits your needs.

Most of our full-timing and extended-traveling friends subscribe to either the AT&T or Verizon one-rate plans. With this type of plan you pay one monthly rate for a given number of minutes. There are no roaming or long-distance charges. This is important to us because we make two coast-to-coast speaking tours every year. A distinct advantage to the one-rate plan is the ability to move from one tier of minutes (and charges) to another once each month. We contract for 1,100 minutes during our on-the-road months and change to 450 minutes when we are at home. Obviously, the cellphone doesn't get much use when we are not on the road.

Vicki: E-mail is the heart of our communication system. We do our best to avoid snail mail and to minimize telephone calls. Our internet service provider is Verizon. They have local-access telephone numbers all over the country. We download all the local-access numbers to a floppy disk once a year. When we arrive at an RV park, it is no problem to look up the local-access number and program our laptop's dialer. There have only been a few occasions when a local-access number was not available and we had to use Verizon's 800 access number. Using the 800 number costs about ten cents a minute, but it is good anywhere, and sending and receiving e-mail doesn't take much time. We also have the capability to go online with our laptop by connecting it to our cellphone.

Joe: We have three computers; a relatively new PC, an old laptop, and a not-so-old laptop. All three use the same word processing program. They are also programmed to use the same Verizon e-mail account. At home, the PC, a printer, and a scanner reside on my desk. The not-so-old laptop and another printer sit on Vicki's desk. The old laptop remains in a briefcase. We take both laptops on the road but the PC stays home.

All of the work we do on our computers is saved to floppy disks instead of the computers' hard disks. That way, as long as we have the floppy disk, the work can be used on any of our three computers. I can start an article on the PC,

Vicki can finish it on the not-so-old laptop, and I can edit it on the old laptop. We can also work on the same project simultaneously. Best of all, this system assures us that if one computer crashes, another can take over.

The lightest and most compact of our three printers stays in the motorhome. We leave the scanner at home. So far, we have not missed it.

All our important file folders fit into one portable file box. Our son, Sean, is a professional cabinet maker. He created a 14 inch by 20 inch file box for our files. The box sits on a slide-out shelf in my desk when we are at home, and next to the driver's seat (and out of the way) when we are in our motorhome. Sean also made a special top for the file box so it becomes a center console, holding coffee cups, maps, sunglasses and other stuff while we are driving.

Vicki: Three overhead cabinets in the motorhome are dedicated to office storage. One cabinet is for the printer, the other two contain a calculator, printer paper and miscellaneous office supplies. The two laptops are stored in drawers under the couch. Originally, our plan was to remove an easy chair from the motorhome and have Sean build a desk in its place. But Joe likes sitting in one easy chair and propping his feet up on the other while working on the laptop, and I am quite content to work at the kitchen table. The printer, when we need it, sets up very quickly at either the kitchen table or on the front passenger seat.

Anything we can't handle with what we have in the motorhome, we can accomplish at Kinkos. They are everywhere.

Moving the "office" between the house and motorhome is simply a matter of transferring the file box, two laptops and a container of floppy disks.

When we are on the road the answer machine on the primary (incoming) telephone line is switched to "toll-saver" operation. The phones on the secondary telephone line have their ringers turned off. We don't want persistent telephone ringing to reveal our absence. The fax machine is also turned off so people don't think we have received and read their faxes.

On the road, we use the cell-phone a couple times a day to check and respond to our telephone messages. Our mail-forwarding person retrieves our snail mail and forwards it to us once a week by Priority Mail. It has never taken more than four days to arrive at its destination.

It took some trial and error but our portable office works for us. Best of all it is simple, functional and relatively inexpensive.

What To Take

My husband and I are getting ready to go on an extended trip in our RV. I'm accustomed to packing the RV for weekends, but I'm not sure what I'll need to take for three months. I'm afraid I'll take too much. And, what kinds of kitchen appliances and household items do folks use in their RVs?

Joe: Try to visualize the places you'll be going and the things you'll be doing. Will the weather be hot or cold; wet or dry? How dressed up will you need to be? How often will you be preparing meals in your RV?

The kitchen utensils and appliances you take with you will depend, not only on the amount of storage space you have, but also on how much cooking you do. We know folks who never use their RV kitchens at all. They eat all of their meals in restaurants. Most of the extended RV travelers that we've met, however, seem inclined to cook in their RVs just as they would at home. You can eat convenience foods for just so long.

During the summer we use our portable barbecue for many of our meals. Cooking outside is one way to keep the inside of the RV cool. During pleasant weather, a barbecue, combined with the range in the RV and a microwave/convection oven seem to satisfy all our meal preparation needs.

During the winter our favorite kitchen appliance is the crock pot. Stepping into a warm RV and the aroma of dinner cooking in a crock pot can be a real treat on a cold winter day.

Once in awhile, with our generator providing the power, we cook in the crock pot while we're traveling down the road. Properly timed, dinner is ready when we arrive at our destination.

Vicki: Another favorite appliance is our pressure cooker. We bought it at an RV show a couple of years ago. It's fast and convenient and is really handy when we're in a hurry.

Rather than a drip coffee maker, we prefer an "old fashioned" electric percolator. Since it is made of stainless steel rather than glass, it's easy to store and we don't have to worry about the glass carafe breaking .

We also use a toaster on a regular basis and, occasionally, an electric mixer.

Our electric skillet comes lets me cook outside when I'm preparing something messy or inside when the range's three burners are not enough

Toaster ovens are a versatile appliance that some RVers just would not be without. They can accomplish a variety of baking and heating chores. And, along with portable barbecues, portable stoves and electric skillets, they allow cooking to be done outside on hot summer days.

Some of the kitchen appliances that we've heard others say they can't live without are blenders, waffle makers and bread machines. Can you imagine traveling down the road with the aroma of baking bread filling your rig? It's certainly possible if you have a motorhome equipped with a generator; but, do you have the storage space for such a large appliance?.

When it comes to clothing, take enough to last seven to ten days and plan on doing laundry once a week. Keep in mind that mix-and-match outfits will help to minimize the amount of clothes you need. Take durable clothing. Commercial washers and dryers can be hard on clothes.

Make sure you take clothing for all kinds of weather. Even if you are convinced that the weather will be warm, take a couple of sweatshirts and a jacket. During our first winter trip to Florida we took only warm-weather clothes. It turned out to be one of the coldest winters in the state's history.

We always have rain gear (including umbrellas) available. You never know when a storm may appear. Joe keeps a pair of slip-on rain boots in our RV. Not only are they handy for going out in the rain, he also uses them when washing the RV or when it's necessary to troop through wet grass or mud to get to the utility connections.

Most RVers dress pretty casually, but it's a good idea to take one dressy outfit for each of you. You'll have a lot more flexibility in choosing restaurants and you never know when a "dressy" occasion may present itself.

We learned about dressy outfits the hard way during a visit with relatives in New England. When we arrived, we found that a family wedding was scheduled to take place. It was our big opportunity to see everybody at one time but we had only brought casual clothes. We had to go out and buy complete new outfits.

Put your dressy outfits in plastic dry-cleaning bags or garment bags and hang them at the back of the closet. Make sure that you also take all the accessories you'll need. Jewelry can be put with shoes and stuck in a corner of a closet or drawer. You may never use these clothes, but at least you will be prepared.

Joe: Equip your RV as completely as possible. Your RV should have its own linens, dishes, cooking utensils, small appliances and other items. This will minimize the amount stuff you have to load and unload before and after your RV trips. If things are permanently stored in the RV, it's unlikely they'll be left behind.

Personal appliances we can't do without and that are permanently stored in our RV include an electric razor, hair dryer and curling iron.

You might want to equip your RV with a small amount of office supplies. This would include pens, pencils, paper, envelopes, postage stamps, ruler, stapler, paper clips and calculator.

Lots of RVers are taking their computers and printers on the road. Laptops take less space and make it easier to send and receive e-mail.

A laundry basket containing soap, bleach and fabric softener should occupy a permanent spot in your RV. If you have the space, add an ironing board and iron. The ironing board could be a table top model. We have discovered that many campgrounds are making ironing boards and irons available to their guests.

Find a spot to store a vacuum cleaner, then buy a vacuum cleaner that will fit into it.

If you are a list maker, list all the items that you think you should take with you. The list should only include the things are that <u>not</u> already stored in the RV. As you load the items into the RV, cross them off the list.

Once you are happy with your list, make several copies. That way, you won't have to make a new list each time you leave on a trip.

Obviously, the most important things on the list will be those items that are absolutely irreplaceable. Irreplaceable items would include prescription medications, reading glasses, cash, credit cards, checkbook and address book.

Vicki: Don't forget to take things to do in your leisure time. Will you be fishing, golfing, hiking? You don't want to forget those golf clubs or that favorite fishing pole. Be sure your checklist includes a camera and plenty of film (film is usually more expensive when purchased on the road).

If you enjoy reading, take a supply of books and, of course, you can always buy more along the way. When either of us is finished reading a book or magazine, we either donate it to an RV park's exchange library or we leave it in the campground laundry room. Somehow, a book or magazine doesn't seem so expensive when you know it will be enjoyed by others.

Keep in mind that as long as you have the irreplaceable things with you, it's not a big deal if you forget anything else. You can always buy another along the way or you can do without.

Trip Planning

How does one go about planning an RV trip? Where do you begin? What do you consider?

Joe: All RVers plan their trips. Some make detailed itineraries. They know what time they will depart in the morning, where they intend to spend the night, and what time they will arrive. Others plan their day so loosely it appears they have no plan at all. They begin their travel day "sometime after breakfast" and get off the road where and when it suits them.

Whether it's detailed or loose, a good trip plan will consider time, distance and money. All three relate to one another. It takes time and money to go the distance.

Begin planning your trip by determining how much time is available. Time is a limiting factor we all have to consider ... time available for the entire trip ... time you will have to devote to travel ... time you want to spend at your destination(s).

Take into consideration that while you may have a three week vacation, you might have to spend two or three of those days packing your RV and preparing it for travel. When you get home, another day or two may be necessary to unpack your rig and get ready to return to work.

The remaining days can be divided between time spent traveling on the road and time at your destination(s). If you are committed to a given number of days at your destination, you will have to plan your travel time according to the remaining days available.

Knowing how many miles you will travel is an important factor in planning a trip. The distance (number of miles) between major cities and destinations can be found on good maps and computer mapping programs. By adding up these distances you can determine how far you will have to travel between each destinations as well as the total number of miles you will drive during the entire trip.

Many of these maps also show the estimated travel time for those distances. Keep in mind, though, that the travel times are for automobiles. RVs will probably take a few more minutes to cover the same distance.

When planning your travel day, figure that you will travel an average of 50 miles per hour. You might set your cruise control at 65 miles per hour, but traffic conditions, road construction and restroom breaks will usually reduce your average speed to about 50 miles per hour.

To calculate how many hours it will take to reach a destination, divide the number of miles to that destination by 50 (average miles per hour). Add to that the time you spend off the road having lunch or whatever and, at the end of the day, you should arrive at your destination within a half hour (more or less) of your estimated time of arrival.

The time you spend traveling each day is an individual consideration but you should consider the safety, comfort, and enjoyment of everyone in the RV. If the driver stays behind the wheel to the point of being fatigued, his alertness and reaction time will be adversely affected. If legs and backs begin to cramp for lack of a stretch break, or if boredom and restlessness has everyone dreading the travel portion of the trip, get a clue, this is not a fun trip. Daily traveling time needs to be adjusted.

Most experienced RV travelers have come to the conclusion that five to seven driving hours a day is about right. At an average speed of 50 miles per hour, that translates to between 250 and 350 miles per day. Occasionally, these RVers will have a longer travel day, but five to seven hours of driving is usually a comfortable compromise between distance and comfort.

Vicki: Money is a serious consideration when planning an RV trip ... money for fuel, food and campgrounds ... money for entrance fees and entertainment ... money for day to day expenses.

Fuel is a major travel expense. Obviously, the more miles you drive, the more money you will spend on fuel. To estimate your fuel expenses, you need to know your RV's average fuel consumption (miles per gallon) and the average cost of fuel.

At the beginning of your next trip, fill your RV's fuel tank and make a note of the odometer's mileage. Fill the tank again when the fuel gauge reaches the one-quarter to one-third full mark. Make a note of the RV's mileage, the number of gallons of fuel it took to fill the tank, and the price per gallon you paid for fuel.

Let's say your starting mileage was 16,000 miles when you first filled the fuel tank. Later, at 16,500 miles you put in 65 gallons of fuel to refill the tank, and you paid $2.00 per gallon.

Subtract your starting mileage (16,000) from your ending mileage (16,500) to ascertain how many miles you have driven (16,500 - 16,000 = 500 miles). Next, to determine how many miles your RV will travel on a gallon of fuel, divide the number of miles driven (500) by the number of gallons (65) it took to refill the fuel tank (500 / 65 = 7.69 miles-per-gallon).

Finally, divide the price of a gallon of fuel by the miles-per-gallon ($2.00 / 7.69 = .26); that tells you how much fuel costs for each mile you drive your RV (26 cents per mile).

You can now estimate that your RV will travel 7.69 miles on a gallon of fuel and at a cost of 26 cents per mile.

Your mileage will vary depending upon driving conditions and your driving habits. Fuel costs will also change slightly from one locale to the next. But, your fuel-cost-per-mile figure (26 cents per mile) will let you approximate how much your fuel will cost on a given trip. Fuel for a 2,000 mile journey, in the above example, would cost about $520.00.

Campground costs vary depending upon the type of campground and facilities you desire. A destination RV resort offering full hookups, golf course, tennis courts, swimming pool, spa, and organized recreational activities is likely to cost $50.00 or more per night. A campsite in a backwoods government campground with nothing more than a picnic table and firepit could cost as little as $15.00 per night. Most campgrounds and RV parks appear to be charging somewhere between $20.00 and $35.00 a night.

Look in your campground directory to research the various types of RV parks and campgrounds and their fees. Don't be afraid to experiment with a variety of overnight accommodations. It's the only way you will discover your own "comfort level".

Some RVers stay in less expensive campgrounds, perhaps with only an electrical hookup on travel days, and in RV parks with full hookups when they reach their destination. Others are not happy unless they can jump into a swimming pool at the end of each travel day. That's the beauty of RVing; you can choose your campground according to your personal tastes and budget.

Your travel expenses will also include food (groceries, restaurants, etc.), admission fees, souvenirs, and all the miscellaneous expenses that travelers incur.

Once you have determined the time you have available for the trip, the distance you plan to travel and what it will cost for fuel, campgrounds and other expenses, it may be time for a reality check. Do you really have enough time and money to cover the distance you plan to travel and to do the things you want to do? You may have to make compromises in time, money or distance.

Selecting Campgrounds

"We bought our motorhome two years ago. Since then we have only stayed in a couple of nearby campgrounds recommended by friends. This summer we want to spend three months touring the country. What criteria should we use when choosing a campground while traveling?"

Joe: It depends upon a number of factors: the amount of time you intend to stay in any one location, the type of facilities you want and, of course, your budget.

We suggest you take advantage of this travel opportunity to experiment with a variety of parks and campgrounds.

Begin by learning how to read your RV park and campground directory. The listings and information it contains will help you select the RV parks and campgrounds that best suit your needs.

You'll find RV park and campground directories at book and RV accessory stores. The directories list the RV parks and campgrounds by area. You simply open the book to the area where you want to stay to find the campgrounds available.

Each individual listing will include information about the campground, its facilities and fees. Owners of large rigs should pay particular attention to the campground's size limitations.

Commercial directories don't always list government campgrounds. Try to obtain listings or directories of the national, state, county and city campgrounds in the areas you are visiting.

Reservations at campgrounds and RV parks should be made according to the location and time of year just as you would at a hotel or motel. If you want to stay on a holiday or summer weekend, reservations might be wise. On the other hand, if you will arrive during the middle of the week or during the off season, reservations may not be necessary.

Many RV travelers prefer to travel without the constraints of an itinerary. They don't make reservations because they don't know where they will be on any given day. Others, with a particular destination and time frame in mind, will secure their campsite by making reservations. RVing offers this freedom of choice.

Generally speaking, RV parks and campgrounds fall into two basic categories; enroute and destination.

Enroute parks are those in which you only intend to spend a night or two while traveling.

When you just want to spend one night in a campground, easy access and convenient site setup will probably be more important than scenic surroundings. You'll also appreciate a campground or RV park that is conveniently close to the highway, yet far enough away to avoid the sounds of traffic.

With any luck the campground will have level, pull-through sites. That will save you the time and trouble of unhitching and leveling.

Will a simple park with basic amenities do the job? We have seen a growing number of no-frills overnight RV parks along the interstates.

Most offer level, pull-through sites with full hookups for as little as $15 a night. Showers and restrooms are usually small and laundry rooms typically nonexistent.

Some may have playground equipment but rarely a pool. Personally, we find these RV parks offer everything we need for a quick overnight stay.

A destination campground or RV park is one where you intend to spend some time. It may be in a national park you wish to explore, on the outskirts of a big city you wish to visit, or adjacent to a lake that needs fishing.

A lot of RVers will select a destination campground in a convenient, central location. This enables them to make exploratory day trips in different directions. We call this "hub-and-spoke" camping.

When you intend to stay at a destination campground for a few days or longer, the size, orientation and surroundings of your site may be more important to you than the time it takes to back, level and hook up to utilities.

Vicki: Consider the availability and convenience of utility hookups, laundry room and other facilities when selecting either an enroute park or destination campground.

Before registering at the campground office, you may want to inspect the facilities that are important to you and your family. I make a point of checking the number and cleanliness of the campground's washers and dryers if I plan on doing laundry while we are there.

Be sure to check the availability of the swimming pool if your kids are looking forward to a swim. The only thing more disappointing than a drained swimming pool is one that is full of water but off limits to kids.

And, speaking of kids, some RV parks are "adult only" but fail to publicize the fact. Read your campground directory listings and their accompanying advertisements carefully. Look for clues that may indicate an "adult only" park. Call ahead if you have any doubts.

We have heard complaints from 50-year-olds about RV resorts with a 55 and older policy. Some parks, on the other hand, make it very clear in their advertising they welcome kids who are under 55 years of age.

Joe: How much do you want to pay? You get what you pay for; or so they tell me. RV resorts usually cost more than the average RV park. Government campgrounds generally cost less than commercial campgrounds.

Most RV parks and campgrounds post their campsite rates on a board behind the registration desk. There may be a basic overnight fee with additional charges for each hookup service. There may also be additional charges for more than two persons, pets, additional vehicles and use of air conditioners or electric heaters.

Some RVers want full hookups every night and are willing to pay for them, others may only request electric and water hookups. They will use the campground's disposal station when they leave in the morning.

Before you register, ask about discounts. Members of RV clubs like Good Sam, Escapees and FMCA frequently qualify for discounts of ten percent or more at many RV parks and campgrounds (this includes some government campgrounds).

Ask about weekly rates. On more than one occasion we have found the seven-day weekly rate amounted to what the daily rate would have been for six days.

While you are registering be sure to ask for:

A pull-through site if you have a long rig.

A site wide enough to accommodate your slide-out room(s).

Hookup connections on the left (driver's) side of the campsite. (That's where your RV's connections are located.)

A shady site in the summer (bird and tree sap droppings may come with it).

A sunny site when it's cold.

A site close to the recreational facilities if you won't mind the noise.

A site convenient to the restroom if you won't mind the foot traffic.

A site near the laundry room if you are going to use it.

We've talked to RVers who prefer the consistent quality and facilities of chain campgrounds like KOA. Others insist the RV parks have a campground directory rating of 7/7/7 or higher and some stick to membership campgrounds.

Vicki and I, on the other hand, like to adventurize. It's not unusual for us to impulsively pull into a park we know nothing about. We've had a few disappointments but we've also discovered a lot of wonderful RV parks and campgrounds around the country.

Experiment. Spend a few days in an RV resort that offers a golf course, tennis courts and organized recreation activities. Dry camp in a government campground. Stay in a variety of commercial RV parks and campgrounds with different ratings and facilities. It won't be long before you develop your own campground selection criteria.

Locating Uncrowded Campgrounds

"We are relatively new to RVing. We often see articles about RV camping in the boonies or see pictures of RVers at some remote body of water. Is this reality? How do you find remote, pristine wilderness to dry camp in while traveling? What other options do we have besides using campgrounds, rest areas or truck stops?"

Joe: We have dry camped on isolated beaches along the Baja Peninsula, on a secluded section of lakefront in central California, on open stretches of desert in Arizona, next to a glacier in Alaska and on a lonely bluff overlooking the coast in Maine. So, yes, it is a reality. But, in all cases, we just happened upon them. In fact, some of our best camping experiences were the result of happenstance. We refer to those occasions as serendipity.

Vicki: You'll find remote dry camping opportunities available on government land administered by the National Park Service, National Forest Service, Bureau of Land Management and the U.S. Army Corps of Engineers. All of these agencies will send maps and information to you.

Keep an eye open for fairgrounds, race tracks, city and county parks. Many of them offer camping or overnight opportunities. We have found camping facilities at wildlife refuges and on land controlled by lumber and power companies.

Joe: If you enjoy uncrowded campgrounds, be contrarians like Vicki and me. We prefer to travel during the off-season months of April, May, June, September and October.

When the snowbirds are heading south for the winter, we are enroute to New England for the fall colors. During holiday weekends when the destination campgrounds are packed, we spend our time in relatively uncrowded enroute parks.

Vicki: Build your own library of campground and RV park directories. You will find them at RV accessory stores. You'll find others are available from federal, state, and county governmental agencies, RV clubs, auto clubs and tourist bureaus.

We routinely stop at every state's welcome center. Most are located in rest areas just as you enter the state. You'll find maps and brochures describing places of interest and things to do. Ask the person behind the counter for directories to city, county and state campgrounds.

We have picked up some of the best leads to great camping spots while talking to fellow RVers in campground laundry rooms.

Joe and I have been RVing for over 40 years. We are still discovering new and exciting places to go and things to see and do. You are just beginning. Think of all the adventures that await you.

Membership Campgrounds

"A lot of people have suggested that we join a membership campground. Will you explain how a membership campground works?"

Joe: Covenants and conditions differ among the various membership campground organizations but here is a very simplified explanation:

When you join a membership campground you become entitled to camp free in that campground, which we'll refer to as your "home campground", for a limited number of days each year.

You are not purchasing a lot or campsite; only the right, as a member, to use your "home campground".

To join, you pay an initiation (or joining) fee in the thousands of dollars. You also commit yourself to paying dues or a maintenance fee of a few hundred dollars each year. By the way, it is only realistic to expect the annual dues to increase periodically.

The cost of joining may also include finance charges and miscellaneous costs.

If the "home campground" is associated with other membership campgrounds, you may be able to stay in any of that association's campgrounds, usually for a camping fee of a few dollars per day.

This "association" privilege may involve an additional initiation fee and slight increase in your annual dues.

Some membership campground associations have an affiliation with other membership campground associations. For an additional joining fee and additional annual dues you may be able to stay in any of the affiliated association's campgrounds. Again, there will probably be a low daily camping fee.

Vicki: RVers join membership campgrounds for a variety of reasons. The camaraderie of belonging to a group, the feeling of being in a secure environment or the assurance of being able to find a campsite are just a few.

The appeal of membership campgrounds to most RVers, though, is the ability to camp in a large number of campgrounds for a low daily camping fee.

If that's your reason for joining, you'll want to be sure the affiliated membership campgrounds will be available to you.

There may be a requirement that in order for you to use an affiliated campground or receive the low daily rate, it has to be located a certain distance, perhaps a hundred miles or more, from your "home campground".

Some RVers buy into a "home campground" located in a distant, remote location so they are able to use the various affiliated campgrounds closer to home.

Also, check to be sure there are affiliated membership campgrounds along the roads you will travel and in the areas you are likely to visit.

There's no point in belonging to a membership campground if you're not going to be staying in their campgrounds.

Joe: Do some math if your objective in joining a membership campground is to reduce your camping expenses. Figure out how many nights you will have to stay in membership campgrounds, as opposed to non-membership campgrounds, to really save money.

Prices vary but let's say, for example, the initiation (joining fee) in a national affiliation of membership campgrounds costs about $6,000 and the current annual dues are $300 per year. Let's also assume you will use the membership for ten years.

The initiation fee ($6,000 divided by 10 years) would amount to $600 per year. The annual dues would add another $300 per year. Using these figures, it would cost $900 per year to maintain a campground membership.

A non-membership campground charges about $30 per night for an equivalent campsite.

Dividing this $30 into the $900 annual cost of campground membership means you could stay in non-membership campgrounds for 30 nights each year for what it would cost to belong to a membership campground.

This computation does not take into consideration the interest you would have to pay to finance the $6,000 initiation fee or the interest the $6,000 would earn if it remained in your bank account. Nor does it reflect the possibility of assessments and periodic increases in annual dues. It also ignores the probability of increased overnight camping fees at both membership and non-membership campgrounds.

But it does give you a formula to determine if belonging to a membership campground would make financial sense to you.

In this case, if you think that during the next ten years you will spend more than 30 nights per year in membership campgrounds, it might make good financial sense to join one.

There's also a possibility (but no guarantee) that you could sell your membership at the end of the ten-year period. That would further reduce the overall cost of membership.

Look at the classified section of RV magazines under "Membership Campground Resales" to get an idea of what people are *asking* for their memberships. Resale competition can be pretty keen.

Vicki: Check out a number of competing membership campgrounds before buying. Visit or, better yet, spend a couple nights in what would be your "home campground". Talk to the members. Ask them if they would recommend joining. Do they have any difficulty making reservations? What is the financial condition of the campground?

Listen to the sales presentations. Ask questions. Take lots of notes.

Membership campgrounds sustain themselves by selling memberships. What is the ratio of members to campsites at the "home campground" you are considering joining? Are non-members, in addition to members of affiliated associations, allowed to camp in your "home campground"? How difficult will it be for you to make reservations in your "home campground"?

Find out if you would be allowed to sell your membership during the first few years of ownership. Are there transfer fees or other costs involved in selling your membership? How many times may the membership be resold? Can it be passed on in your estate?

How do you cancel your membership? What are the financial ramifications if you stop paying the annual dues?

What happens to your membership in the affiliated campgrounds and associations if your "home campground" goes bankrupt? Will you lose your investment?

Take home, scrutinize and compare the literature and copies of the contracts.

Joining a membership campground should complement your RVing needs, make financial sense and enhance your enjoyment of RVing.

Investigate before you invest.

Self-Contained Camping

"We recently bought a 32-foot motorhome and have thoroughly enjoyed staying in RV parks with hookups. This fall we plan to visit a number of national parks where we will be camping self-contained for the first time. Do you have any advice that will make "roughing it" easier?"

Joe: You're going to discover that while most of the campgrounds in government parks may not offer utility hookups, they do have waste-water disposal stations and drinking-water hydrants. "Roughing it" means the inconvenience of taking your RV to these facilities when it becomes necessary.

When you stay in most of today's commercial RV parks or campgrounds, chances are you enjoy the convenience of utility hookups. A water hose connects the RV's plumbing to the campground's water supply. An electric cord brings in campground power. A sewer hose empties the rig's waste water into the campground's sewer system.

Hookups may even be available for cable TV and, if you're really lucky, there may be a telephone hookup. All the comforts of home while away from home.

Pull into a government campground, however, and you'll probably have to rely upon your rig's self-containment features.

Nearly all of today's RVs come equipped with self-containment features. An on-board storage tank carries fresh water. A "gray-water" holding tank captures waste water from the shower and sinks. A "black-water" holding tank collects toilet waste. One or more 12-volt batteries supply electrical power. A propane tank provides fuel for cooking, heating and to operate the refrigerator.

Self-containment capacities vary from rig to rig but most RVs will allow you to camp comfortably for at least two to three days without hookups.

Vicki: Seasoned RV campers have learned to extend their "dry camping" time by practicing conservation and expanding their RV's self-containment capabilities.

Here are some of their secrets for successful dry camping:

Conserve water. The less water you use, the fewer trips you'll have to make to the local water hydrant to refill your RV's water tank.

One obvious way to conserve the RV's fresh-water supply is to take advantage of the campground's restroom and shower facilities whenever possible.

If you do use your RV shower, take a "navy" shower. Use a minimal amount of water to get wet, turn off the water, soap yourself and then use only enough water to rinse off.

Don't let the water run while brushing your teeth or while washing your hands and face.

Use paper plates to reduce the number of dishes that have to be washed.

Wash dishes only once a day. Instead of pre-rinsing, use paper towels to wipe leftover food from the dishes.

Some RVers recycle dishwater by saving it (in a bucket or plastic jug) for flushing the toilet.

Minimizing the amount of water you consume means you'll also be conserving holding tank space.

There are not many RVs whose gray-water tanks equal the capacity of their fresh-water tanks. Since the sinks and showers drain into the gray-water tank, it's not unusual for some RVers to run out of gray-water holding-tank space long before they run out of fresh water.

Black-water tanks that capture toilet waste, however, are frequently larger than necessary.

With this in mind, one way you can save gray-water tank space is to wash dishes in a plastic dishpan and empty the dishwater into the toilet and its black-water tank. Some RVers even capture shower water and dump it into the black-water tank.

A covered waste-water collector, such as a Tote-Tank, can be connected to the RV's sewer outlet to capture gray water. Depending upon their size, Tote-Tanks can collect up to 30 gallons. They even have wheels that make it easier to take them to a campground's disposal station.

Joe: Conserve battery power. Most RVs come equipped with a Group 24 deep-cycle battery. This battery has a capacity of about 80 amp-hours of electricity.

A single 12-volt ceiling light bulb draws about 1.5 amps; a 9-inch color TV about 3 amps; and the furnace fan 7.5 amps while operating. Obviously, the less amps you consume, the longer your battery will last. So turn off unnecessary lights and keep 12 volt appliance operation to a minimum.

Check your 12-volt RV light fixtures. Many are equipped with two bulbs. Experiment to see if one bulb will do the job.

Consider replacing one or two 12-volt incandescent light fixtures with fluorescent ones. They consume less electricity and provide more light.

When it's time to replace the coach battery, buy a Group 27 deep-cycle battery. Its 105 amp-hour capacity is 30% greater than the Group 24's 80 amp-hours.

If one deep-cycle battery isn't sufficient for your needs, see if it's possible to install a second one. It's best to install two identical new batteries at the same time rather than simply connecting a new battery to your existing battery.

Check into the possibility of installing two 6-volt golf-cart batteries in your coach. Wired in series for a 12-volt output, the batteries will have a capacity of about 230 amp-hours.

A generator will provide 120-volt household power and slowly recharge your batteries.

If it won't disturb your neighbors, think about running your generator just after you get up in the morning and again around dinner time. This will allow you to take full advantage of all the electricity it produces. In addition to operating your lights, you'll probably be able to run the microwave, electric coffee pot, hair dryer, vacuum cleaner and other appliances.

Many RVers have installed solar systems in their RVs. The good news about solar power is, it really works. The bad news is, the equipment can be expensive. Do some research. A solar system could be a practical investment depending upon the amount of time you spend self-contained camping.

Vicki: Conserve propane. Keep in mind that the water heater and forced-air furnace are among the greatest consumers of propane.

Instead of allowing the water heater to cycle on and off all day, turn it on just once a day to heat water for showers and washing dishes. It takes only 30 to 40 minutes to heat the tank. Then you can turn it off for the remainder of the day.

If you only need enough hot water to do dishes, heat water in a tea kettle on the stove. That way you avoid turning on your water heater and heating six to ten gallons of water.

Better yet, fill up the kettle with hot water at the campground's restroom.

Another way to reduce propane consumption is by installing a catalytic heater. It uses considerably less propane than the other propane heaters and, unlike the fan of a forced air furnace, it doesn't use electricity.

Joe: When the RV's lights are dim, the water tank is empty and the holding tanks are full, you'll know it's time to move.

If the campground has a disposal station and a drinking water hydrant, "roughing it" will amount to moving your RV to the disposal station, dumping the waste water, refilling the fresh-water tank and returning to your campsite.

Or, you can move down the road and check into an RV park or a campground that offers electric, water and sewer hookups. The drive will probably recharge your batteries.

While there, you can refill your water tank, empty the holding tanks and take advantage of the 120-volt electricity to use your vacuum cleaner. Chances are they will also have a laundry room.

Experiment. Keep your eyes and ears open. You'll discover a number of ways to stretch your RV's self-containment capabilities.

Your RV can provide you with all the comforts of home while away from home. Take advantage of its versatility.

Visit the government parks, stay in friends' long driveways and be sure to enjoy the full service facilities of the commercial RV parks and campgrounds.

The self-containment features of your RV are made to order for enjoying our government parks and campgrounds. You're heading for a great adventure!

Cold-Weather Camping

"We want to explore the mid-Atlantic states during January, February and March. Our travels will take us into freezing temperatures and light snow. How should we prepare our rig? Do you have any suggestions for winter camping?"

Joe: It's no secret to experienced RVers that cold weather months can be a great time to travel and camp in an RV. Traffic is lighter, campgrounds are uncrowded and the weather is stimulating.

Today's RVs are insulated, have efficient heating systems and provide a snug refuge from foul weather. Soup, coffee and hot chocolate are quickly prepared on the kitchen stove.

Comfort lovers can enjoy the luxury of curling up on the couch with a good book while others take advantage of outdoors activities. Clothing to match the changing weather is conveniently available in closets and drawers.

Prepare for the cold-weather season by draining and backflushing the engine's cooling system. Experts recommend a 50% water and 50% antifreeze mixture in the radiator to give you protection to 34 degrees below zero. This is also a good time to check the heater hoses and heater operation.

Engines demand more electrical starting power during cold weather. Check the battery's electrolyte level, clean the terminals and coat them with petroleum jelly.

Don't forget to lubricate the chassis and change the oil on your engine and generator. Check your owner's manual to see what grade of oil is recommended for the anticipated temperature range.

Check the condition of the windshield wiper blades and the operation of the windshield washer. Fill the reservoir with windshield washer fluid. By the way, windshield washer fluid contains methanol and won't freeze.

You'll want a set of tire chains if you think you'll encounter snow and ice. Practice putting them on while it's warm and dry.

Fill the propane tank. This will minimize condensation inside the tank and help prevent vaporization problems in cold temperatures.

Vicki: Your RV's built-in space heating system should be adequate for keeping the interior warm. Keep in mind, however, that a forced air furnace will not only consume propane but up to seven amps per hour of electricity as well. This could represent a considerable drain on the coach battery if no hookups are available.

You can reduce consumption of propane by augmenting the propane furnace with a portable electric heater. Be sure the RV hookup cord and any extension cord to the heater have a sufficient amperage rating to withstand the wattage of the heater. Divide the heater's maximum wattage by 120 (volts) to determine the minimum amperage rating of the electrical cord. (A 1,500 watt heater would require an electrical cord with a minimal rating of 12.5 amps.)

Many RVers who do a lot of self-contained camping use catalytic heaters. Catalytic heaters combine propane and oxygen over a platinum-impregnated pad. The chemical reaction releases energy in the form of radiated heat. It requires no electricity and utilizes propane more efficiently than a forced-air heater.

Most catalytic heaters are not vented to the outside. They consume oxygen from inside the RV and should only be operated when open windows can provide ventilation. A window and a roof vent, each open 18 square inches, should provide adequate ventilation for a 6,000 BTU catalytic heater.

Look for ways to improve your RV's ability to retain heat. You can block the cold radiated by a motorhome's windshield by hanging a heavy blanket between the driver's compartment and the rest of the coach.

Heavy drapes or curtains will insulate the coach windows against the cold. An insulating dead air space can be created by covering the inside of the windows with clear, heavy vinyl. Some RVers use sheets of Styrofoam to cover the interior of their windows.

Roof vents can be covered on the inside with Styrofoam or snap-on vinyl covers. Throw rugs, especially on vinyl flooring, will add insulation to the floors. They'll also protect the carpeting against tracked in dirt and moisture.

Weather-stripping around entry doors and exterior cabinet doors will prevent cold drafts.

Styrofoam or fiberglass insulation can be attached to the inside of exterior cabinet doors.

Joe: You'll want to examine your rig's plumbing to determine what measures may be needed to prevent damage from freezing temperatures.

The fresh-water tanks, water pump, pipes, drains, holding tanks and dumping valves of some RVs are protected by locating them in heated channels or compartments. The heat source is one or more ducts from the forced-air furnace. As long as the furnace runs periodically, the water in the pipes and tanks shouldn't freeze.

Other RVs, however, may have their drains, holding tanks and dumping valves below the floor and exposed to outside temperatures.

Empty the holding tanks if they will be subject to freezing and pour a couple of quarts of non-toxic, biodegradable antifreeze into each holding tank. This will protect the dump valves. Pour in more antifreeze as waste water fills the tanks. Pouring the antifreeze into the gray-water tank through the shower drain will also protect the drain pipe below the shower.

When outside temperatures approach freezing, disconnect, drain and store the drinking water and sewer-hookup hoses. Slightly opening the doors of interior cupboards that contain plumbing will allow heated air from the coach to circulate around the pipes.

Drain the water system if you are unable to protect the fresh-water pump or plumbing from freezing. Even better protection is provided by using compressed air to blow the remaining water from the pipes or by simply pumping non-toxic, potable antifreeze throughout the water system.

Some cold-weather RVers winterize and then don't use their plumbing system at all. Instead, they carry containers of drinking water inside the living area of the RV and rely completely upon the campground's restroom facilities. Call ahead to the campground if this is your plan. Some close their restrooms during the off season and others may only provide electrical hookups.

Vicki: You can use electric tank heating pads and electric heating tape to protect plumbing when you stay in a campground or RV park that provides electrical hookups.

We have used electric drop cords to protect plumbing in exterior cabinets. The heat from the lightbulb was sufficient to keep things from freezing.

Hot water and ordinary electric heating pads can be used for thawing out frozen hoses, pipes and valves. Our favorite tool is the hair dryer. We once used a hair dryer to melt ice from our TV antenna so it could be lowered for traveling.

Wherever you go during the fall and winter months be prepared for sudden drops in temperature. We were enroute to sunny Mexico one February and ran into freezing temperatures in Tucson, Arizona.

Before driving into an area on a dirt road, consider what it will be like to drive out on that road when it is slick from rain.

Try to camp in a spot that is open to the heat of the sun and, if possible, protected from the wind. You can minimize cold drafts by facing the RV into or away from the prevailing wind.

Keep in mind that snow accumulating on overhanging branches may eventually drop off in heavy clumps or perhaps bring down the brittle branches. Don't let snow block the refrigerator roof vent.

Cold-weather camping doesn't necessarily have to include freezing temperatures and snow, but be prepared for occasional rain and some cold weather. And don't be surprised if you find yourself in an almost empty campground experiencing warm, balmy weather.

Your RV is, in all likelihood, built for cold-weather camping. All you need to add is common sense and perhaps some antifreeze and snow chains. And don't forget the hot chocolate!

Locating Dump Stations

We are concerned that we may not be able to empty our holding tanks when we need to. Is there a guide or list of disposal stations?

Joe: Smart travelers never leave a restaurant or other public building until after they visit the rest room. Smart RVers never leave a campground until after they empty their holding tanks. You just don't know how long you will have to wait before another facility becomes available.

But, every once in a while, you find yourself on the road and in need of a dump station.

Look in the front section of your *Trailer Life Campground, RV Park and Services Directory*. It lists the locations of rest area equipped dump stations along the interstates.

If the rest areas along your travel route do not have dump stations, the TL Directory will also help you locate RV parks and campgrounds located near the highways. Most commercial RV parks will let you use their dump station for a fee. If a commercial campground is not available, look for a government campground. We have found dump stations available in most state and county campgrounds. Some have charged us a day-use fee, others have just waved us in.

Don't overlook the state and county fairgrounds. They usually have dump stations, but some fairgrounds are not always open.

Check out the truck stops and travel plazas. A book titled *The RVers Friend* lists truck stops and rest areas with dump stations. Flying J Travel Plazas are on interstate highways all over the United States. Most of them offer free dump stations at their RV fuel islands. You can pick up a map of all their plaza locations at their fuel desk.

Some RV dealerships and repair facilities have dump stations. They may be listed in the TL Directory and you will certainly find them in the yellow pages of the telephone directory.

If the need becomes urgent call a septic tank service. You may be able to dump where they do, or maybe they will pump out your holding tanks.

Try to locate a dump station close to your residence. Make it your last stop before going home.

Vicki: Please be considerate when using these facilities. A large number of dump stations across the country have been closed due to ill-mannered RVers.

Position your RV so the holding tank outlet is located above the dump station's apron. That way, if there is any spillage, it will be directed toward the drain. Connect one end of your sewer hose to the RV and insert the other end into the dump station receptacle. Be sure the hose remains in the receptacle until your tanks are through draining.

After emptying your holding tanks, close both their valves. Don't put anything into the dump station except the contents of your holding tanks. Use the appropriate water faucet and hose to rinse your sewer hose and to wash off the dump station apron. Make room as soon as possible so the next RV can dump its holding tanks. Always try to leave the place better than you found it.

Safety And Security

"Do you feel safe out there? Do you carry a gun?"

Joe: What these folks are really asking is, *"Aren't you afraid of becoming a crime victim?"* and *"What can we do to protect our valuables and ourselves?"*

Our standard reply is that we feel just as safe in our RV as we do at home. Maybe safer.

It would be foolish to think that we are completely safe while RVing. Nothing is completely 100 percent safe.

Actually, life is full of risks. House fires occur every day; yet you sleep in a house most nights. Automobiles are constantly involved in accidents; but you continue to drive every day. An earthquake or meteorite could suddenly destroy the building you're in; but there you sit.

These are a sample of the risks we acknowledge, accept and deal with every day of our lives. Life is full of risks.

Traveling in an RV also has risks; we wouldn't attempt to tell you otherwise. But we will tell you that when you are RVing, you are living in a relatively low-crime neighborhood.

Before we look at that neighborhood, let's look at the criminal. As with everything, there are exceptions and extremes but, generally, the criminal is an opportunist looking for an easy target, a fast grab and a quick getaway.

Think about it. The burglar prefers to take your valuables when you aren't there to protect them; the petty thief steals when you're not aware of his presence and the con artist strikes when he can take advantage of your ignorance. The purse snatcher, mugger and armed robber rely upon force or fear to control their victims.

Whatever their mode of operation, all of these criminals select an easy or vulnerable target. They move quickly and make their escape as soon as possible.

Obviously, the criminal would prefer to pass over a target that is difficult to control or could result in him getting hurt or caught.

Vicki: Now let's look at the RV neighborhood. Generally speaking, the RVer is not an easy target subject to a fast grab.

RV destinations and campgrounds are seldom located in what would be considered high-crime areas. Oh, we have stayed in a few big city RV parks with security patrols and fences topped with barbed wire but they are few and far between. One of the appeals of most RV destinations is the fact that they are located in relatively low-crime areas.

RVers generally park in close proximity to other RVers. And there always seems to be at least one couple sitting outside who seems interested in everything that's going on around them. Non-campers are pretty easy to spot and, as a result, they attract attention to themselves.

And you never know when a ranger, camp host or strolling camper will pass by. These are people who could come to an RVer's aid or act as witnesses. Criminals prefer to avoid the inconvenience involved with getting caught.

It's difficult to establish patterns of movement or occupancy in and around RVs. We come and go unpredictably. You can't be sure if the RV occupants are gone and you never know when they will return. That person walking up the road might be the owner of that RV, his friend or the campground owner.

It's also not easy to determine who, what or how many may be inside an RV. It could be a lineman for the Rams, a snarling Great Dane or a little, old lady with a big, new gun. Criminals have the same aversion to pain as everyone else.

And, an RV, because its windows are higher off the ground, can be more difficult to break into than a house.

As you can see, RVers, by virtue of their lifestyle, do not present an easy target for a quick grab and a fast getaway.

Joe: There are some common sense things you can do to further minimize the risks of becoming a crime victim

Harden the target. Install good locks and get in the habit of using them. If you don't already have one, put a deadbolt lock on your RV's entry door. Upgrade the locks on the exterior storage bays.

By the way, it's not a bad idea to re-key your factory-installed deadbolt lock. There are a lot of master keys floating around. And, of course, you should have a locksmith re-key the deadbolt and other locks whenever you purchase a previously owned RV.

A hitch lock will discourage anyone from hooking up to your trailer and driving away.

Back up the latches in sliding windows by placing metal or wooden rods in the channel at the base of the window.

Use a light chain or cable to secure bicycles, barbecues and other outdoor items to the picnic table or RV bumper.

Store your cash and valuables in a hidden safe or lockbox inside your RV.

Install exterior lights that can be turned on from the interior of your rig. Use manual, not sensing, lights. Sensing lights go on and off all night. Your neighbors either ignore them or soon begin to hope that you do get robbed.

If you install an alarm, advertise the fact, and spend the extra bucks for one you can personally activate if you need help.

A dog that barks when strangers approach (but only when strangers approach) is a great deterrent.

Vicki: Avoid becoming a target. An RVer can be vulnerable when his rig suffers a roadside breakdown, especially at night. The risk of a breakdown can be minimized with a good program of preventative maintenance. The only way to completely avoid breaking down at night, though, is to travel during daylight.

Carry a cellular phone so you can call for help in an emergency. Stop by the welcome center of each state you visit. Ask what number you should dial on your cellular phone in case of an emergency. While you are there, pick up a state map. Most state maps will list the telephone numbers you can call in an emergency.

Know where you are. Develop the habit of knowing your location. Help will arrive a lot sooner if you can tell the police dispatcher your highway number, direction of travel (northbound, southbound, etc.) and the nearest milepost marker or exit number.

Keep in mind that using your CB radio to call for help also notifies everyone else of your situation and location.

It's a difficult judgment call as to whether you should get out of your disabled rig when a stranger stops and offers to help. One option is to stay in the safety of your vehicle and ask the stranger to call the Highway Patrol or your emergency roadside service.

Be wary of strangers telling you to stop because your RV has a problem. Drive to the nearest occupied rest area to check for RV troubles.

Traveling with other RVers gives you safety in numbers and the security of someone to help you during any type of problem.

Avoid any place where you do not feel comfortable or your intuition tells you is unsafe, especially when you're considering spending the night.

Camp within eyesight of other RVers. Make a point of saying "hello" to neighboring campers. They will be more inclined to pay attention to strangers around your rig.

Don't show off computers, cellular phones, wads of cash or other tempting, easy to steal items.

Draw the blinds at night. There's no point in revealing who and or what is inside your RV.

Don't put a sign on your rig advertising your name. That makes it easy for someone to knock on your door and call out your name(s) as though you were acquainted.

Don't open the door without visually checking out callers. Talk to them through an open window.

Be wary of strangers who want to see the inside of your rig because they're "thinking about buying one".

Put a light on a timer and play a radio when you are gone; just like you do when you are home. And don't leave notes saying you're not in the campground and when you'll return.

Generally speaking, when you are RVing, you are in a low-crime neighborhood. Use common sense, listen to your instincts and you can further reduce the risks of becoming an easy target for a fast grab and a quick getaway.

Joe: People we don't know frequently ask if we carry a gun in our RV. I'm concerned that if I answer "yes", they may be tempted to steal it, and if I answer "no" they will think we are a vulnerable target. So, I politely respond, "If you really want to know, kick in my door and step inside".

Everyone then assumes I am a bloodthirsty, gun-loving, redneck just itching for an opportunity to blow someone's head off. An image I don't agree with but see no point in discouraging.

There's a lot of discussion these days about carrying a gun in an RV. I'd like to contribute my observations. The purpose of a gun is to kill. If you're not prepared to take someone's life, perhaps you should think twice about carrying a gun.

Police officers receive hours and hours of professional training on the use of deadly force. And they occasionally make fatal mistakes. If you do decide to carry a gun, please take a thorough training course on how and when to use it. More importantly, learn when <u>not</u> to use it. After all, I might be parked next door to you some night.

By the way, if you decide to carry a handgun in your RV, familiarize yourself with the handgun laws of the cities, counties, states and nations you plan on visiting.

Vicki: Generally speaking, the RV world is a low-crime neighborhood. Obviously, Joe and I feel quite comfortable out there. Our comfort level comes from knowing that RVers are generally not perceived as targets of opportunity.

We also use common sense to avoid becoming crime

victims. And then, there's this odd perception people have about my husband that he sees no point in discouraging.

What's In Your Wallet?

Losing a purse or wallet can be twice as devastating when you are traveling. Next time you are near a copy machine, make a couple copies of your driver's license, credit cards, insurance cards and any other important papers in your wallet.

Make a note of the telephone numbers you should call if your credit cards, etc. are lost or stolen. Store one set of the copies in your safe at home and another in a safe place in your RV.

If you do lose your wallet or purse, you will now have the information you need to cancel the lost credit cards and arrange for duplicates of your other documents.

Guns N' RVs

We are about to take our first cross-country trip in our RV. We will camp in a variety of State and National Parks but will probably camp most frequently in commercial campgrounds with hookups. We have guns in our home and I think I would feel safer if we had one in our RV. What do you think?

Joe: We Americans have a love affair with firearms, especially handguns. Firearms have put food on our tables, protected our families, and freed us from tyranny. It is estimated that the majority of American homes have at least one firearm. We collect them, hunt game with them, and keep them for self protection.

It only stands to reason that if you own a firearm you might want to carry it in your RV. Before you do, however, there are some things you should consider. Is it legal? Is it necessary? Is it practical?

Let's begin with the legal issues. Most states, counties and municipalities have laws that restrict carrying firearms on your person or transporting them in a vehicle. The laws pertaining to handguns are usually more restrictive. It only makes sense to find out if it is legal for you to possess, carry and/or transport your particular handgun, rifle or shotgun in your own home state and community. You should also determine the legal method for transporting that firearm in a vehicle in those locations. Many states require the firearm to be unloaded, cased, and kept in a locked compartment that is not accessible to the driver and passengers while the vehicle is on the highways.

But, being legal in one state doesn't mean you will be legal in another state. Just because your state allows you to carry a firearm on your person or in your vehicle (either with or without a permit), don't expect the same privilege in other states.

Federal law generally permits individuals (with some exceptions, such as felons, and a few others) to transport firearms from one place where that person may legally possess and transport those firearms, across state lines to another place where that person may legally possess and transport those firearms. The firearms must be unloaded, in a locked trunk or (if the vehicle does not have a trunk) in a locked container other than the glove box or console while they are being transported.

It seems reasonable to believe that this law includes the brief times one must stop to fuel while enroute. It also seems reasonable to believe that state and local laws would take precedence once the transporting individuals end their travel day by stopping at a motel or pulling into a campground. If you are going to transport a firearm across state lines you would be well advised to research the laws of the states and communities where you intend to spend one or more evenings, especially if you are transporting a handgun.

A good resource for firearms laws in the United States, Canada and Mexico is the National Rifle Association

RVers traveling with firearms face further restrictions. National Parks generally prohibit firearms. National Forests typically follow the laws of the state in which they are located. State Parks vary but usually prohibit or restrict firearms. Make inquiries before taking a firearm into these types of destinations.

Canada requires a special permit in order to bring handguns across their border. "Firearm Declaration" permits are required to bring "sporting" rifles and shotguns into the country for target competition or hunting purposes. Call 1-800-731-4000 for more information.

Mexico prohibits handguns and makes it extremely difficult to legally bring hunting rifles and/or shotguns into their country. Possession of illegal firearms, or even ammunition, is illegal. Violators go to jail.

Many RVers, in spite of the laws, carry firearms somewhere in their RVs. "How often" they will ask, "do you hear of an RV being searched by the police?"

Generally, RVs are not often the subject of a police search. That's probably because we have an image of being law-abiding citizens who seldom commit more than an occasional traffic violation.

Searches of RVs, however, do occur. Police officers who arrest drunk drivers and other criminals frequently "inventory" the contents of the suspects' vehicles before having them towed to an impound lot. Searches are conducted at Canadian and Mexican border crossings (both coming and going). And searches take place at U.S. Border Patrol check points located on highways north of the Mexican border. Searches of RVs do occur.

Vicki: Is it necessary to carry a firearm while RVing? RVers can be victims of crimes, just like anyone else. But when you are RVing, you are in a relatively low-crime neighborhood.

RVers, you see, generally do not present easy targets of opportunity for criminals. We typically spend the night in campgrounds where our neighbors are located in close proximity. People in campgrounds spend a lot of time outside where they can witness unusual activity. Our RVs are difficult to break into. And, until the door opens, it is not easy to determine who, what or how many are inside an RV. These factors all have a strong crime-deterrent effect in the RVing environment. Ironically, there is another possible crime deterring element. RVers have the reputation, deserved or not, of carrying guns and being willing to use them.

RVers who make a habit of camping among other campers, locking their doors and using common sense seldom encounter criminal activity. Needing a firearm for self protection should not be any more necessary while RVing than it is when you are at home.

Finally, is it practical to carry a firearm in an RV? Unless you want to risk getting caught with an illegal weapon, you may have to avoid stopping in some states and countries you would like to visit. And let's face it, a firearm, unloaded, cased, and locked in a cabinet, is not going to be readily available for self defense.

Keep in mind that using a firearm for self protection is only justified in a life threatening situation. If you do decide to have a firearm for self protection, or for any other reason, be sure to take a professional training course so you will know how, when and, most importantly, when not to use it.

Traveling With Pets

"We want to travel in our RV with our two dogs. Any advice?"

Joe: A lot of RVers take their dogs, cats and other household pets on the road. Vicki and I frequently see RVs with two or three dogs and/or cats.

We have even shared campgrounds with dog-sled enthusiasts. These folks travel with a half-dozen or more dogs. The animals are very well behaved and their owners set an example in campground etiquette we wish other pet owners would follow.

Most RV parks and government campgrounds accept dogs and cats. There are some, however, that have restrictions on the size and breeds of the dogs they will allow onto their property. Owners of Pit Bulls, Dobermans, German Shepherds and the like might want to call ahead and ask if their dog is welcome.

Don't be surprised if there is an extra charge for your pet. You may even be assigned to an area of the campground designated for pet owners. The campground will ask you to clean up after your pet, keep it on a leash and not allow it to disturb your neighbors. RV pet owners who think these rules do not apply to them are the reason some RV parks and campgrounds now refuse to allow pets.

Vicki: Some dogs and cats, like human beings, readily adapt and even look forward to RV travel while others have difficulty adjusting.

Keep in mind, your animals will be barraged by new sights, sounds and smells. They will be in close contact with a variety of strange people and surroundings. This can be stressful for some dogs and may lead to barking and unpredictable behavior.

It may be a good idea to accustom your pets to RVing by taking them on short trips at first, then gradually increasing the length of time they spend on the road and in campgrounds.

Try to locate a permanent place in the RV for the animal's food and water bowls.

Provide a protective travel case for your pets. It will keep them from jumping on or otherwise interfering with the driver. It will also prevent them from becoming flying missiles when the brakes are suddenly applied. The travel case can double as a familiar and secure place for your pet to sleep.

Joe: You'll want to carry a valid rabies vaccination certificate. Many government campgrounds and some RV parks require them. RVers traveling to and from Canada and Mexico are required to have a valid veterinarian health certificate, including a proof of rabies vaccination.

Be prepared in case your dog or cat gets away from you. Put an identification collar on it. Include your RV's make and license number as well as your RV's cellular phone number. You might ask your veterinarian about identification tattoos and under-the-skin implants. Check into the lost pet service offered by RV clubs.

Carry a leash for exercising and some type of tethering rope or chain to keep your pet within the confines of your campsite.

By the way, don't leave your animal tethered and unattended outside the RV. Unable to flee, it would be easy prey for a wild animal. And you certainly wouldn't want your dog to attack a child who suddenly ran through your campsite.

Vicki: Think about what you will do with your pet when you are not able to take it with you for the day. You don't want to leave it unattended in a hot or unventilated RV. A vent fan or air conditioner can be left running, but what if there is a power failure?

Some campgrounds and recreation destinations offer "day-care" kennels. Before you drop your pet off for the day, inspect the premises. Ask what protective measures they take against parasites, infection and distemper.

Take care of your animal's health. Mosquitoes transmit heartworm. Ticks and fleas abound in outdoor areas. Ask your veterinarian about preventatives.

Be aware that strange food and water could cause digestive upset. This is not the time to alter your pet's diet.

Pet odors can build rapidly in the confined space of an RV. You'll want to work diligently to minimize odors and prevent fleas.

Finally, be a good neighbor. Clean up your pet's waste. Keep it on a leash. And please, don't permit it to bark, whine or otherwise disturb the RVers around you.

RV Travel Tips

"We have only used our travel trailer for weekends and vacations at nearby campgrounds. This summer we want to spend our three-week vacation traveling around neighboring states. This will be our first RV travel trip. Any helpful tips?"

Vicki: The best time of year to travel is during the "shoulder" months of May, June, September and October. These months experience mild weather and less travelers throughout most of the country.

The best weekends to travel are just before a holiday weekend. Everyone is getting ready for the holiday.

The best days to arrive at a campground are late Sunday and anytime Monday. All the weekenders will have just left and there will be plenty of sites available.

Plan your trip using detailed road maps with time and mileage indicators. Automobile clubs are excellent sources of good maps. We've found that traveling in an RV generally takes about ten percent longer than the time indicated on maps.

Use a highlighter pen to mark your route on the map. When choosing your travel route, try to avoid the heavy traffic of big cities and the engine strain of steep mountain passes.

Every major population center has its "rush hour". Select your route and time your travels to avoid getting caught in commuter traffic. Don't overlook the possibility of heavy weekend traffic if you travel late Friday or Sunday afternoons.

Joe: Most RVs are designed to maintain a comfortable highway cruising speed of 55 miles per hour. Many RVers drive faster but, by the end of the day, most generally average 45 to 50 miles per hour. So, no matter how fast you drive, when planning your travel day, figure that you'll average 45 to 50 miles per hour on the main highways.

Seasoned RV travelers have discovered that driving between four and six hours each day is a much more comfortable pace. It allows them to stop at interesting spots, enjoy a leisurely lunch and arrive at their destination in a relaxed frame of mind.

While an occasional long driving day is OK, try to keep your actual driving time to less than six hours per day. It may take some attitude adjusting, but you and your family will enjoy your travels a lot more.

Drive during the early hours of the day. Your mind is fresh and clear. Driving into the morning sun is less brutal than driving into the afternoon sun. You'll avoid the heat of the day and winds will be less of a problem. Driving through hot deserts and up mountain grades during the cool early hours of the day is also easier on your rig's engine.

Take a break every couple of hours. Walk you rig. Look underneath for leaks, check the condition of your tires, be sure the trailer hitch and connections are secure.

Vicki: Make your lunch break a fun part of the travel day. Roadside rest areas are convenient, but a city park or playground will be a treat for the kids. Historical sites have plenty of parking space and give you an opportunity to stretch your legs. We like to combine lunch with a visit to a local tourist attraction or a factory that offers tours.

Lunch is also a good time to open your campground and RV park directory, look ahead and line up a couple of overnight camping destinations. If your first choice doesn't work out, you'll have an alternative.

Stop at each state's welcome center. Look for them in rest areas as you cross from one state to the next. Welcome centers usually have racks of informative brochures that have been placed there by commercial interests, tourist attractions and campgrounds.

Joe: Check out a travel plaza when it's time to refuel. Once known as truck stops, travel plazas are courting the business of RV travelers. Travel plazas offer gasoline and diesel fuel, convenience stores, restaurants and restrooms. Many have even installed dump stations and easy-access RV fuel islands.

Plan on getting off the road by four or five in the afternoon. RV parks and campgrounds will have more vacancies. There'll be time to go for a walk, take a swim or treat yourself to a nap.

Vicki: Take advantage of the campground laundry rooms. RVers have a tendency to chat while waiting for their clothes to wash and dry. They can tell you their impressions of campgrounds, attractions and road conditions they have encountered.

Some of the best travel tips and money-saving advice we've received has come from RVers we've met in campground laundry rooms

Washing The RV

Do you have any tips for dealing with the millions of suicidal bugs that attack the front of my RV? And how do RVers wash their motorhomes and trailers when they are on the road for long periods of time?

Joe: At the end of each driving day I use a boat brush on a telescoping handle and half a bucket of plain cold water to wipe (notice, I didn't say wash) the bug remains off the windshield and front wall of our motorhome. The carcasses seem to come off easier when they are removed on the day of impact.

Most campgrounds, citing environmental regulations, drainage concerns, or water shortages, prohibit washing RVs in their campgrounds. There are some, however, that do allow their patrons to wash their rigs, either in individual campsites or a "wash rack" area. A few even provide a vacuum cleaner. We make a note of these RV parks and return to them whenever we are in the area.

Sometimes, the operators of the campgrounds that prohibit washing of RVs may be able to direct you to a local do-it-yourself car wash that can accommodate an RV. Wouldn't it be nice if they included that information along with the printed rule prohibiting washing of rigs in their campground. Occasionally, you'll see these car washes advertised in the campground's site map.

Vicki: Before taking our RV to one of these car washes we use our car to check it out. We want to be sure our rig can maneuver into and out of the wash bay. The RV usually gets washed the next morning after we check out of the campground and before we resume our travels. It's not unusual for us to end up paying for two car washes in order to completely wash our motorhome.

Speaking of the campground site maps ... we have seen ads in them by professional RV wash crews who will come to your campsite. Typically, they use a high-pressure water hose that does a long-lasting job. Interestingly, some of the campgrounds that prohibit their patrons from washing RVs in their campsites will allow a professional wash crew to do the job. Go figure. The wash crews have charged us between $1.00 and $1.50 a foot and, so far, have always done an excellent job.

Be careful here, though, some RVers have told us that the high pressure hoses can peel the stick-on graphics and decals off the RV.

Commercial truck washes can be found along the interstates; frequently in the neighborhood of a truck stop (or travel plaza as they are now called). Most, if not all, will wash RVs. We make a habit of asking before getting into line. Typically, they use high pressure hoses along with mops, brushes and detergents. We've paid anywhere from $1.00 to $1.75 per foot to have a commercial truck wash do our motorhome.

Joe is a tightwad. He prefers to wash our motorhome himself (sometimes he lets me help). But, every now and then he treats himself and lets the professionals do the job.

Watch The Truckers

You used the phrase "Watch the truckers" in one of your RV seminars. What, specifically, should we be watching?

Joe: You can learn a lot by watching the truckers. Watch how they handle their rigs, maneuver through traffic, and help one another move down the road.

Pay particular attention as they make their turns. Observe how far from the curb they are when making a right turn and how far they pull into the intersection before actually beginning a turn.

Watch as they back their rigs. Notice how they position the backs of their trailers before backing up to a loading dock or into a parking space. Notice, too, they are not afraid to use a forward gear during the backing process.

Watch how truckers use their lights. Many of them drive with their headlights turned on during the daytime. This is a safety practice that makes them more visible.

Observe how truckers flash their lights when one overtakes and passes another. The trucker being passed will flash his headlights on and off when it is safe for the passing truck to return to the driving lane. The passing trucker will activate his right turn signal, move to the driving lane and then flash his running lights on and off as a way of saying thank you to the trucker he just passed. This courteous behavior keeps a lot of trucks from bumping into one another as they travel down the highway.

Before you decide to engage in this signaling practice, however, you should be aware there may be some liability on your part if you signal to a truck that it is safe to change lanes and it results in an accident. And don't forget how many trucks are driving with their headlights on during the daytime. You do not want to move back to the driving lane after passing a truck just because you see that truck's headlights in your mirror. Learn to use your mirrors to accurately gauge when it is safe for you to make a lane change.

Speaking of mirrors, have you noticed the size, type, number and position of the mirrors on those big trucks? Professional drivers spend a lot of time paying attention to the traffic lanes on both sides of their rigs. They are also interested in where the rear of their trailer is in relationship to those lines painted on the road. A big truck's mirrors will extend out far enough to allow the driver to see the entire side of his trailer. There will also be at least one large convex mirror on each side to help him see what is in that blind spot just behind his cab doors. Truckers know, and RVers soon learn, that little "four-wheelers" seem to gravitate towards that blind spot.

Vicki: Keep an eye on the traffic lanes selected by the majority of truckers. Chances are they have driven this road before and know which lane will get them to their destination with the least amount of hassle. And when you see a number of trucks in front of you suddenly changing from one lane to another, you might want to do the same. Another trucker has probably just alerted them by CB radio of a road or traffic condition up ahead and they are moving into the best lane to get around it.

Listen to the trucker channel on your CB radio. It is channel 19 in most places. Truckers will use their CB radio to alert oncoming drivers to road hazards, traffic accidents and slowed or stopped traffic (they call it a brake check). There have been a number of occasions when we have been able to select an alternate route, jump off the interstate and avoid a traffic jam by paying attention to these trucker advisories.

Listening to the trucker's channel can be entertaining; truckers can tell some funny stories. It can be enlightening; you will learn a lot about truckers and the trucking business. It can also be scary; you will come to realize there are a few truckers and trucks (as well as RVers and RVs) that shouldn't be on the road. Hopefully, that awareness will keep you driving defensively.

Watch the truckers. There's a lot you can learn about driving and getting along on the road. Try to do what the professional drivers do, but please don't follow the example of the few "hotdoggers". And give the truckers a break. Remember, they are under pressure to deliver a load. Give them room; room to get on the highway, room to change lanes, and room to pass. Watch out for the truckers and you'll soon realize that, given the opportunity, they'll watch out for you.

Trucker Talk

What in the world are the truckers talking about? We are new to RVing and this is the first time we have had a CB radio. For the life of me, I can't seem to decipher half of what the truckers are saying to one another.

Joe: I happen to like listening to the CB radio while we are traveling. I particularly enjoy listening to the truckers. I consider that prime time entertainment.

Channel 19 seems to be the most popular CB channel for truckers across the nation. They use channel 17 along the west coast and, occasionally, we pick them up on 21.

Truckers in the west are not very talkative. You don't seem to hear from them unless they have something to say. East of the Mississippi, however, truckers get real chatty. They talk to one another about anything that comes to mind; sometimes without even filtering it through their mind. That's the entertaining part.

Listening to truckers is also educational. You gain some insight into their lives and what it is like to move those big rigs around the country. You learn that truckers work long, hard hours. They deal with a lot of pressure, boredom and frustration. You also come to realize that, while most have a professional approach to their driving, there are a few immature hotdoggers out there that have no business pushing 80,000 pounds of steel and cargo down the highway.

I learned a long time ago that truckers use the CB to advise one another of road and traffic conditions. Their advisories, more often than not, apply to RVers as well. If there is a traffic situation that has blocked one or two driving lanes, truckers will radio which lanes are open. This information allows us to change lanes before traffic begins to back up. When there is an unexpected road closure, truckers will broadcast directions to alternate routes. We have avoided time consuming traffic jams on more than one occasion by paying attention to the truckers.

So, yes, we listen to the CB radio as we drive. It keeps us tuned into the road. And, every now and then, we enjoy a conversation with a trucker who also happens to be an RVer.

Vicki: Truckers have developed their own colorful terminology. It took a while for us to learn what they were talking about.

Many State Police officers and Highway Patrolmen wear a hat similar to the one we see on Smokey The Bear. That's why the terms "smokey" and "bear" are used when talking about police officers who patrol the highways.

Truckers seem almost paranoid about the State Police and Highway Patrol, and are constantly updating one another about their location. I love the way truckers differentiate between the various types of "bears". A "full-grown" bear is a State Police officer or Highway Patrolman. Since one of their primary duties is to police the highways, truckers are particularly interested in their whereabouts. A "county mountie" is a local Deputy Sheriff. They may or may not be interested in truckers and seem to command a little less respect than the "full-growns." A "local yocal" is a city police officer. A local yocal is rarely interested in enforcing traffic laws on interstate highways but truckers keep a wary eye on them anyway. A "plain-wrapper" is an unmarked patrol car. "Polar bear" refers to a white patrol car. A "bear in the air" is a police helicopter or airplane. A "she bear" or "mama bear" is ... you guessed it ... a woman police officer. And, my favorite, a "kojac with a kodak" refers to a police officer using a radar gun.

When a police officer has a vehicle pulled over to the side of the road he has "captured" that driver. A lot of "capturing" activity will bring out the expression "there's bears everywhere" or "they got us surrounded"

Truckers apply their own descriptions to the vehicles sharing the road with them. A "four-wheeler" is a car (a constant source of annoyance to truckers); "stagecoach" is a bus; "bread truck" is a motorhome, and "draggin wagon" a tow-truck.

And, they have names for their own as well. A "covered wagon" is a flatbed or open trailer with a tarp cover. A "parking lot" is a car transporter. And we have heard truckers refer to their sleeper as a "condo".

They call weigh stations "chicken coops" (a closed coop is cause for celebration). So now you know where the "chicken inspector" works.

You've seen those strips of tire tread lying on the road. Truckers call them "alligators". If your wheel rolls over an alligator, it has a tendency to jump up and attack your vehicle. The highway department trucks that remove these road hazards arc known as "alligator catchers"

When a trucker warns of a "brake check", he's talking about an unexpected slowdown in traffic (brakelights everywhere). Get ready to slow down or stop.

The "hammer lane" is the far left fast lane. That's where you can put your "hammer" or accelerator down (providing that Smokey isn't around)

If someone (or something) is "in the bushes" they're off the side of the road and pretty much out of sight until you get close to them. Bears like to hide in the bushes.

"Yard line" or "yard stick" refers to the mile markers at the side of the road. If something is located at the "20 yard line" it is near the 20-mile marker.

There are a few more terms that I can't mention here. But if you turn on your CB radio and listen to the trucker talk you can hear and figure them out yourself.

So, the next time you hear a trucker call out, "northbound, you've got an alligator in the hammer lane", you'll be able to take evasive action. And if they tell you there's a "kojac with a kodak in the bushes at the 32 yard line", it's your own fault if you get captured.

Interpreting the Interstates

Joe: Knowing how the interstate numbering system, its mile markers and exit numbers work can be a valuable tool for the RV traveler.

The numbers on the interstate signs provide information about your location, direction of travel and distance to your destination. Interstate numbers, mile markers and exit numbers are frequently used on road signs, billboards and radio station advisories. And knowing the numbering system will help you furnish directions when you call for roadside or emergency assistance.

Interstate highways are described as traveling either east and west, or north and south. There may be areas where an interstate does not run exactly due east/west or north/south. But the main direction that most of the road travels is the one used to describe it.

The east/west interstate routes have one or two digits and are even-numbered. Beginning with the lowest interstate number (I-4) in Florida and progressing to the highest interstate number (I-94) across the northern tier of the United States. Interstate numbers ending with a 0 are long distance, usually transcontinental routes.

The north/south interstate routes have one or two digits and are odd-numbered. The lowest north/south interstate number (I-5) is on the west coast. The interstate numbers get progressively higher to the east. The highest (I-95) is on the east coast. North/south interstate numbers ending with a 5 are generally long distance routes.

There are also shorter, three-digit interstates. Three-digit interstates either connect or branch off other interstates.

If the first digit of a three-digit interstate is an even number, it usually connects to another interstate at both ends. These highways are frequently in the shape of a loop or beltway. (I-495 around Washington, DC for example)

If the three-digit interstate begins with an odd number (I-395 into Washington, DC), it is usually a "spur" highway from an interstate and might not connect with another interstate (most do, however).

The last two digits of a three-digit interstate indicate the major highway it is connected to (I-495 connects to I-95, both north and south of Washington, DC).

Now you know - if you are on an even-numbered interstate you are traveling either east or west; if you are on an odd-numbered interstate you are traveling either north or south. And if you are on a three-digit interstate, you might be going in a circle.

Vicki: So how can you tell which direction you are going? Interstate highways have mile markers. They are those little green signs located on the right side of the highway. The signs have a number and possibly the word "mile" written on them.

On one and two-digit interstates the mile markers show how many miles you are from either the state line of the state in which you are traveling, or from the location where the interstate originates within that state.

Mile markers on north/south highways begin counting from the state's southern state line. Mile markers on east/west highways begin counting from the state's western state line. So mile marker numbers get higher as you travel north or east. When you cross the state line into another state, the mileage numbers start over again.

Traveling east on Interstate 10 in Texas, mile-marker 1 is one mile east if the western state line. The mile-marker numbers get higher until you reach the state line of Louisiana. As soon as you cross into Louisiana, the mile markers will start with Mile 1 again.

Driving north on I-35 in Texas the mile markers start at Mile 1 one mile north of the Mexican border and get higher until you cross into Oklahoma where the mile markers begin at Mile 1 again.

When an Interstate highway originates within a state (I-20 in Texas for example) the numbering begins at the southern or western location where it begins (in this case, at I-20's junction with I-10).

So now you know that if you are traveling on an even-numbered interstate and the mile-marker numbers are getting higher, you are heading in an easterly direction. If the numbers are getting smaller, you are heading west.

Similarly, if you are driving on an odd-numbered interstate and the mile marker numbers are getting larger, you are going in a northerly direction. If the numbers are getting smaller, you are headed south.

The three-digit interstates that form a complete loop (circle) around a city have mile markers that are numbered in a clockwise direction. The numbers begin just west of the spot where an interstate meets the southernmost point of the loop. I-465, for example, is a 53-mile loop around Indianapolis. Mile marker 1 is just west of where I-65 intersects the southernmost point of I-465's loop. Mile marker 53 is just east of this same intersection.

Joe: Knowing the interchange and exit numbers makes it easy to change from one highway to another or to exit the interstate. Most states number their interchanges and exits. Some will match the interchange and exit number to the nearest mile-marker number. Exit 12, for example, will be very close to mile-marker 12. If you are looking for Exit 12 and you have just passed mile-marker 10 you know your exit is only two miles away.

A few states, however, number their interchanges and exits consecutively without linking them to the mile markers. In other words Exit 12 may be the 12th exit from the border; but not necessarily at the 12-mile mark. Look at a map to determine which system is being used to mark the interchanges and exits. Better yet, pay attention to the mile markers and exit numbers to see if they match.

Vicki: Knowing the Interstate numbering system simply amounts to this:

Even-numbered Interstates go east and west.

Odd-numbered Interstates go north and south.

When you enter a state from the south or west, the mile markers (and usually the exit numbers) will begin with 1 and get higher as you travel.

When you enter a state from the north or east, the mile-marker numbers (and usually the exit numbers) will be high and get smaller as you travel.

Visiting Big Cities

We are planning our first cross country trip. We especially want to visit the big cities (Boston, New York, Washington, DC, etc.) but I really don't relish the idea of driving our transportation vehicle into congested areas. Are there campgrounds close enough to the major cities with easy connections to buses or trains so we can visit without having to drive our own vehicle?

Joe: I have the greatest respect in the world for the truck and bus drivers who make their living by maneuvering their big rigs through narrow, congested city streets. Personally, though, I do not relish the challenges presented by hostile drivers, suicidal pedestrians, one-way streets, hidden and/or misleading directional signs, and outrageously priced parking lots. When it comes to visiting the cities, my motto is "Take the bus, leave the driving to them".

Vicki: Joe has a tendency to hold things in. What he is trying to say is that we have visited most of our country's major cities by staying in RV parks and using public transportation. Actually, while towing our car with our 36-foot motorhome, he has done a remarkable job of negotiating the downtown areas of a number of big cities. Of course, he could have avoided those experiences if he had just paid attention to my directions.

When we visit a new city of any size we take a two or three day approach. The first day we take at least a half-day guided tour of the city. Professional tours take you to the city's main attractions, point out interesting places to go and give you an overview of the city.

We use the tour day to scope out the city and determine the places we want to go on subsequent days. From then on we take public transportation into and out of the city.

Cities like Boston and Washington, D.C. have excellent commuter trains that take you into the heart of the city. Once there, you can buy an all-day ticket that allows you to get on and off a combination transportation/tour-bus system. One of these, in Boston, is called The Bean Town Trolley. A number of these trolley-looking vehicles travel a loop route among the tourist highlights of the city. Your all-day ticket lets you get off and spend as much time as you wish at any of the stops. When you are ready to continue, you get on the next trolley that comes by. The "trolleys" in Washington, D.C. make stops near all the Smithsonian buildings, National Monuments, and government buildings. They even go to Arlington National Cemetery.

There are some places, though, like Philadelphia's Historical Area, or New Orleans' French Quarter, where parking is not that difficult and most of the points of interest are within walking distance.

Joe: Use your Campground Directory to locate the RV parks and campgrounds that cater to the city tourists. Their advertisements will emphasize their proximity to the local attractions and point out how they can make your visit a pleasant one. A number of them will have public transportation at their entrance or within a short walking distance. Quite a few will provide shuttle service into town. Some will offer their own tours. Many of them will arrange for the commercial tour bus companies to pick you up at the RV park and drop you off at the end of the tour. And the campgrounds that want you to come back and/or recommend them to your friends will have maps, brochures, train and bus schedules, and will spend time helping you plan your visit.

When we visit Boston we stay at Normandy Farms in Foxboro, MA. They offer a variety of tours, and the commuter train station is just a few minutes drive away. In Washington, D.C. we stay at Cherry Hill Park in College Park, MD. This place has its own bus station right on the grounds. The commercial tour buses and public transportation buses pull right into the RV park. What more could you ask for? And the commuter train station is just a couple miles away. The train goes directly into the tourist area of Washington DC. The personnel in both of these parks, by the way, go out of their way to be helpful, friendly, hosts. It's obvious their managers know what it takes to be a success in the hospitality business.

Do a little research. Use your campground directory. Call the campgrounds. Visit their web sites. Take a tour. Use public transportation. You may find, once you are familiar with a city's layout, that you'll even try driving your own transportation vehicle into town.

Alaska - Caravan or Solo

We are going to take our RV to Alaska next summer. This will be a once-in-a-lifetime trip so we want to see and do as much as possible. Would you recommend that we go on our own (we are experienced RVers) or go with an RV caravan?

Joe: Vicki and I have traveled in all 50 states and a good part of Canada and Mexico. As far as we are concerned, traveling through Canada and into Alaska is the ultimate RVing adventure.

Our first RV trip to Alaska was done on our own. We spent more than a year researching, planning and preparing for what we thought would be a once-in-a-lifetime adventure.

The trip lasted three months. We took the Alaska Highway one direction and the ferry system the other. Guided by books, maps, brochures, and the advice of folks who had gone before us, we thought we had seen everything Alaska had to offer. We had a great time.

Then we signed on as "tailgunners" with an Alaskan caravan. The typical RV caravan staff consists of a wagonmaster couple and an assistant wagonmaster couple. While the wagonmaster team is responsible for keeping the caravan running smoothly, the assistant wagonmaster couple, sometimes known as "tailgunners," travel behind the last RV so they are available to assist any caravan members who experience any problems.

The Alaskan caravans followed the same route, went to the same places, and took the same tours we did on our solo trip... plus a whole lot more! And they did it a lot more efficiently. That's their business.

Vicki: An RV caravan company researches the route, puts together the itinerary, makes campground reservations and arranges interesting tours. You travel in the comfort of your own rig with the knowledge that nothing will be missed along the way. You also enjoy the camaraderie of fellow caravaners and the sense of security that comes from traveling with a group.

Once you have signed on, and long before the departure date, the caravan company provides you with maps, daily itineraries, checklists and other information to help you prepare for the trip.

The first day or two of a caravan is usually spent getting acquainted, inspecting vehicles and making last minute preparations.

Each day during the trip begins with a briefing by the caravan staff. They will tell you about the road conditions, scenic attractions and points of interest you can expect during the coming day's journey. Your tour map and itinerary will probably point out fuel stops, restaurants and shopping opportunities.

A typical day's journey will rarely exceed 200 to 300 miles. Most caravan companies encourage their participants to travel solo or with just one or two couples, stopping where and when they please, with everyone coming together at the end of the day. Some caravans, however, travel together in a convoy with everyone starting and stopping in the same place at the same time. It has been our observation that most RVers prefer to travel solo or with one or two other RVs. This might be something to ask about when choosing your caravan company.

As the caravan progresses, you can expect to experience planned events such as river rafting, fishing trips, tours and barbecues.

When you arrive at each day's destination you will be guided into your reserved campsite. But the day won't be over yet. Evening activities will probably include restaurant meals, salmon bakes, potlucks and professional entertainment.

Some Alaska caravans either include or will make arrangements for you to load your RV on a giant ferry, occupy a stateroom and cruise the Inside Passage on your return trip to the US/Canadian border. We happen to think that this should be a part of everyone's Alaska experience.

To learn more about RV caravans, contact the commercial caravan companies. You'll find them advertised in most RV publications. Ask what you can expect to receive for your money. Compare what each company offers on similar caravans.

Once you've experienced the benefits of professional preparation, experienced guides and adventurous companions, you may find yourself joining the ranks of those for whom caravanning has become an addictive form of travel.

Joe: On the other hand, it's only realistic to recognize that caravanning is not for everyone. The positive aspects of caravanning for some can be perceived as negatives by others. Campground reservations and transportation schedules require adherence to itineraries and travel agendas. Shared laughter and adventure involves group participation. The security and comfort of group travel calls for consideration and compromise. If you are independent-minded, accustomed to solo travel and prefer to avoid strict itineraries, you might want to seriously consider whether you'd be happy traveling with a caravan.

Traveling to Alaska on your own is an adventure but no longer a challenge. Most of the highways are two-lane, paved with gentle curves and easy grades. You will also find occasional stretches of gravel with their attendant dust or mud.

Prepare your rig just as you would for any long (5,000 or more miles) journey. Be sure the drive train, suspension system and coachworks are all in good working order. Tires should be less than five years old and have at least half their tread life. One spare tire for each vehicle should be sufficient.

Fuel, towing and repair facilities are rarely more than 60 miles apart. Most accept major credit cards. Auto parts stores and mechanics can be found in most communities.

Pack a week's worth of casual, practical clothing. Jeans, sweatshirts, and long-sleeve shirts will get the most use. Bring rain gear and boots, warm jackets and sweaters, and be prepared for warm days in the interior.

Campgrounds are plentiful. Your campground directory will list a good number of them.

Most commercial campgrounds will have at least one washer and dryer. And you will find plenty of Laundromats in every town along the highway.

Every community has grocery stores and shops. Large towns will have supermarkets and malls.

Do your homework. Research. Plan your trip carefully. Allow six to eight weeks to see and do all that interests you.

Thousands of RVers travel to Alaska on their own and do just fine. You will too!

Making Money On The Road

"Is it possible to generate some kind of income while traveling?"

Joe: We're seeing more and more RVers who are combining their love of RV travel with making money on the road. While many are fulltimers, some are extended RV travelers who live in a house between their income generating trips.

These RVers find ways of making money either as independent business people or by working for others. There's no reason why you can't be one of them.

First, look at your objectives. Think about why you want to make money on the road. Do you need to make a living or just supplement your existing income? Do you want to offset your travel expenses or are you simply interested in making a casual dollar?

Next, sit down with your travel partner and decide how much time and effort you wish to devote to making money. Try to strike a balance between the time you spend working and the time available to enjoy your travels.

Finally, ask yourself what you want to do to make money on the road. Do you want to be in business for yourself or work for others?

Vicki: Being in business for yourself means you have the freedom to choose your working location, atmosphere and hours. You are in control. You are the boss.

Being in business for yourself also means investing the time and money to establish your business. You'll have to deal with business permits, sales taxes and insurance. You may also have to deal with late payments, bounced checks and collections. And then there's the paperwork ...

Do some research. Your local library is loaded with books about starting a home-based business. And that, essentially, is what your "on the road" business will be.

Starting and operating an on-the-road business is the same as any other business but RVers have a few additional considerations.

You'll be conducting business in different locations. Ascertain whether you or your business will require a professional license, sales permit or special certification from local government agencies in each new location. Repeating this procedure and expense every time you move could be prohibitive.

It's a rare business that is not dependent upon a telephone. Telephone hookups are not commonplace in RV parks so plan on using a cellular phone. Get a telephone calling card for the occasions when you need to use a pay phone and don't overlook the money saving potential of pre-paid phone cards.

A telephone answering machine at home or some sort of voice-mail service will be a necessity.

Joe: Research who your customers will be and how you will contact them while you are on the road.

One way to reach customers is to rent a vendor's booth at the thousands of trade shows, fairs, rallies and flea markets that take place around the country.

We have seen RVers selling RV accessories, crafts, wooden signs, custom name badges, herbs, antiques and even flagpoles in these vendor booths.

We are acquainted with one fulltiming couple who supplement their retirement income by selling windchimes at RV shows, rallies and fairs. They carry their inventory and display materials in their motorhome's storage bays. Sometimes they set up under the awning of their RV; other times they set up inside a vendor's building or tent. Years of trial and error have helped them develop a circuit that takes them to the fairs and shows that provide the best income.

If you're going to sell a product, decide how and where you will receive, transport and store that product while you're on the road. Keep in mind that heavy or bulky items may exceed your RV's carrying capability.

Providing a service is one way to avoid inventory and sales taxes. If you presently have a service business, see if there's a way you can take it on the road.

We met a woman who specialized in doing portraits of couples standing in front of their RVs. She took Polaroid photos of them in campgrounds and worked from that. Most of her customers were so pleased with her work, they asked her to do portraits of their grandchildren or pets.

Are you an entertainer? Musicians, magicians, mimes, clowns and ventriloquists find work at trade shows, fairs and special events all around the country.

Vicki: You may be among the many RVers who prefer to avoid business headaches by working for someone else. You will receive a regular paycheck and may even qualify for employee benefits. Best of all, you will only be committed to a pre-determined type of work for an established period of time.

There seem to be more job opportunities available for RVers than there are RVers willing to fill them. Most of these jobs are temporary or seasonal in nature. That means you will have plenty of opportunity to enjoy your travels between jobs.

Commercial campgrounds and RV parks frequently hire RVers, especially during their busy seasons. Jobs include office work, security, recreation and maintenance. Many of the opportunities are for couples. Compensation, in addition to a salary, usually includes a free campsite and discounts at the campground store.

National parks concessionaires hire thousands of RVers every year to operate their hotels, gas stations, grocery stores, gift shops and restaurants.

You'll find openings for tour guides, drivers, maintenance workers, accountants, personnel clerks, computer operators, managers, medical, hotel and restaurant people.

Seasonal jobs are not limited to the great outdoors. The gambling casinos around the country hire RVers as dealers, change makers, security guards, cooks, waitresses, musicians and entertainers.

Pumpkin patches and Christmas tree lots hire RVers. They typically pay a weekly salary and provide a water and electric hookup for your RV right there on the lot. No long commute here.

During the Christmas season, RVers find work as department store Santa Clauses, sales clerks and gift wrappers. And, somebody must paint all those attractive decorations on the store windows.

When you're tired of spreading joy and cheer at the end of one year, you can find work as a tax preparer during the first few months of the next year.

Being an RVer is actually an advantage when looking for seasonal work.

Lots of RVers make a living, supplement their existing income or offset their travel expenses. Either by being in business for themselves or working for others. They are making money on the road. They are making their dreams come true. You can too!

Working On The Road

"We will soon retire and hope to RV fulltime for a few years. Initially we will travel to all those places we have been reading about. Then we plan to locate a new retirement home by staying in selected communities and working for a few months at a time. Can you tell me about getting temporary work while fulltiming?"

Joe: It sounds like you are taking a logical approach to enjoying your retirement. We've talked to a number of people who, like you, want to travel extensively for a while but then re-establish their roots.

Getting a temporary job will not only augment your retirement income, it will give you an opportunity to become a part of the community to see if it fits your retirement needs.

Finding temporary work while fulltiming is not difficult. In fact it appears there are more jobs looking for RVers than there are RVers looking for jobs.

Commercial campgrounds and RV parks frequently employ RVers during their busy seasons. Jobs include office work, security, recreation and maintenance.

Compensation often includes a free campsite with hookups and a salary commensurate with the type and amount of work you will be doing. Since most of these jobs are temporary or seasonal in nature, you will have plenty of opportunity to explore the country between jobs.

One nice thing about working in campgrounds, you are there during the most pleasant time of the year.

Once you have gained some experience working in a campground or RV park you'll find your services in demand almost everywhere you go.

Vicki: Check out the temporary help agencies. Temporary help agencies are no longer limited to clerical or office positions. These companies now find temporary positions for men and women of all ages in every conceivable field.

Accountants, assembly-line workers, bank employees, draftsmen, engineers, executives, nurses, paralegals and pharmacists are just a few of those who can find work through a temporary help agency.

Here's a tip: Establish a good track record with a temporary help agency that has offices nationwide. When you are ready to move to the next community, ask the agency to FAX or e-mail your records to their office closest to your destination. You'll have your paperwork done and a good recommendation waiting when you arrive. They might even have a job lined up for you.

Joe: Don't overlook the general employment market. Scour the want ads, contact the local chamber of commerce, check out the bulletin boards at colleges and local libraries.

Search the trade and professional magazines for ads and ideas. See if anyone is looking for vacation relief or work overload personnel.

Vicki: America is a beautiful country. Its going to be difficult deciding where you want to settle down. So enjoy the search for your new retirement home. But be careful. You may find a new career while you're at it.

RV Show Vendors

"My husband and I recently attended an RV show being held at a county fairground. We noticed a number of RVs that appeared to be camped in one section of the parking lot. Who were these people?"

Joe: The RVs may have belonged to some of the show's exhibitors and vendors. A good number of the folks who set up a display or sales booth at an RV show are RVers. They are among the thousands of RVers who have found a way to make money on the road.

Typically, the vendors arrive the day before the show opens. Display materials and/or sales merchandise will be unloaded from a travel trailer's tow vehicle, the storage bays of a motorhome or, in some cases, an equipment trailer being pulled by a motorhome. The balance of the day is spent setting up their booth or display. The vendors live in their RVs right there at the RV show.

The vendors hope to make enough money during the show to cover their travel and living expenses, pay for the rent on their booth space, recoup their investment in merchandise and, with a little luck, make a profit.

They know their fortunes depend upon the professional skills of the show promoter, the mood of the crowd, the whims of the weather and their own ability to attract and convince customers to buy.

Vicki: While a few vendors are casual sellers of merchandise, most are serious business people. They know which shows and promoters are likely to bring them the greatest return on their investment. Many work a circuit of shows and rallies that keep their down time to a minimum.

Don't be surprised to see a vendor pass your credit card through a card reader connected to a cellular phone. This is the twentieth century and they are very much a part of it.

At the end of the last day of the show the vendors break down their displays and store them in their vehicles. Some may even head down the road that evening. They have another show ahead of them.

Talk to a show vendor during a quiet moment. He may give you some insight into his lifestyle. You might even find yourself the owner of a gadget you never knew you needed.

Missing The Grandchildren

My husband and I, after years of tent and trailer camping with our kids, just bought a new trailer. We're retired now and I'm looking forward to traveling and seeing the country. But, I'm concerned about being away from my grandchildren for a long period of time. I don't want them to think that we don't care about them. And I certainly don't want the toddlers to forget who we are.

Vicki: Just keep in touch while you are gone. In this communication age, there are many ways to stay in touch with kids, grandkids and (for those of us in the sandwich generation) parents. Obviously, each of us has a little different situation, but we can give you some ideas that work for us and other RVers.

Our first grandchild, Amanda, was just a toddler when we took a three month trip to Alaska. I wasn't happy at the prospect of missing three months worth of growth and development. And, I certainly didn't want Amanda to look at me like a stranger when we got home. During that trip, we called our sons and daughter once a week. After talking to my daughter, I always asked her to hold the phone up to Amanda's ear. I made a point of speaking to her in the same upbeat tone of voice. I tried to get Joe to do the same, but no way was he going to carry on a one-way telephone conversation with a baby (it must be a guy thing).

I kept up that baby talk on those weekly phone calls during the entire trip. When we got home, I called to Amanda using the same tone of voice that she had heard in my telephone calls. She smiled and came right to me. Joe didn't get the same friendly greeting. He was a stranger and had to work at making up for lost time with her.

Joe: I still wasn't convinced, but when our grandson, Kevin, was born I went to the pay phones with Vicki and carried on a one-way conversation with him. When we got home, Kevin recognized both of us. The next two grandchildren, Danny and Nicole, received the same kind of phone calls. As a result, Gram and Papa received enthusiastic greetings upon their return home.

We call home at least once a week. Sunday evening seems to work best for everyone. After we talk to our kids we always ask to talk to the grandkids. We make a point of asking them what they're doing, how school is going, etc. The grandkids know they can count on the regular contact and it keeps us up to date on their activities. Sometimes they're not home - sometimes they're playing and they just don't want to talk. That's okay, they know we'll catch them the next time.

We also try to send a postcard to each of our grandchildren every week. We pick age-appropriate cards (animals are always a hit with little kids – location shots for the older ones). It turns out that we are real "mail symbols". The kids all know that when we're gone, they're gonna get mail! The little ones carry their postcards around at home and take them to school to share. Our daughter-in-law started a photo album of postcards that we have sent to Kevin. He now has eight years worth of postcards from all over the United States, Canada, Mexico, and Europe. He really enjoys them.

Vicki: E-mail is another great way to keep in touch with grandkids. We e-mail the older children telling them where we are and pointing out highlights of the area. Now that we have a digital camera we also send pictures that we think will be of interest to them. And they e-mail photos to us. One of our favorites was a proud smile with a missing tooth.

At birthday time, we use our camcorder to make a "Happy Birthday" video. We show our RV in the setting that we're in at the moment, and we position the camcorder to record us talking and singing "Happy Birthday." If nothing else, the kids will roll their eyes and laugh. We also try to find interesting things to add to the video. Last February we made a video to send to our youngest grandson on his sixth birthday. Joe got a shot of me feeding sea gulls in Myrtle Beach. Our grandson really enjoyed that video. Nothing brightens up a birthday like watching a flock of very aggressive sea gulls attacking your grandmother for a crust of bread. On a couple of occasions we have received a video of the face of the birthday child as he or she watched the video we made for them.

We have joined the countless RVing grandparents whose grandchildren visit them while they are traveling. The children fly to wherever the grandparents are located, spend some time and then fly home. We prefer to have one child visit at a time. That way we can tailor the trip to fit his or her individual interests.

You don't have to be home all of the time to enjoy your grandchildren. Think of the interesting experiences that you'll have to share with them. As long as you keep in touch on a regular basis, they won't forget you.

Familiar Places

"Don't you miss the comfort of familiar surroundings when you're away from home?"

Joe: Until you asked the question, we thought the reason we traveled was to escape our familiar surroundings. We thoroughly enjoy discovering and exploring new places and getting acquainted with new people. But, now that we think about it, we do find ourselves gravitating to the comfort of familiar surroundings all over the country.

The nationwide chains and franchises have allowed the entire United States to become our neighborhood.

Vicki: We know, for example, that the quality and type of facilities at KOAs all over the country is pretty consistent. We can count on finding fuel islands reserved for RVers at Flying J Travel Plazas and we know that Camping World stores can repair or service our rig.

We find Wal-Mart and K-Mart stores just about everywhere we go. It's an unusual mall that doesn't have a Sears, Radio Shack and a Hallmark shop. Kroger and Safeway markets offer familiar comfort when grocery shopping and we have also gotten to know the regional favorites like the Fred Meyer stores in the northwest.

Joe: We go to Kinko's and Staples for office supplies and business services; Home Depot and Ace for hardware items; Napa and Kragen for auto parts.

My favorite neighborhood places have names like McDonald's, Cracker Barrel and Lone Star Steak House. And when I'm in the mood for international cuisine we look for Pizza Hut, Taco Bell and International House Of Pancakes.

Vicki: So, you see, we are never very far from the comfort of familiar surroundings but we still enjoy discovering and exploring that corner grocery store or the mom and pop shops. They just seem to add to the adventure of being an RVer.

Information To Go

"Where can I go in my RV? What is there to see and do? How do I get there?"

One of the keys to successful RVing is knowing how and where to get the answers to these questions.

A variety of information sources are available for avid RVers. Here are a few to get you started.

Campground and/or RV Park Directory - A campground directory is a basic RVing necessity. It provides an easy-to-follow system of maps and alphabetical listings which enable you to identify the overnight facilities located in the area you wish to stay.

Each campground listing provides the name, phone number and directions to the campground from the nearest main highway. A description of the campground, its facilities and fees helps you select the one suited to your needs and budget. Finally, a rating system gives you an idea of the quality, completeness and cleanliness of the facilities.

Some campground directories, like *Trailer Life's Campgrounds, RV Parks & Services Directory*, provide additional information such as state highway laws regulating RVs, bridge, tunnel and ferry restrictions as well as the locations of disposal stations along major highways.

Most RVers travel with two or three different campground directories.

RV Magazines - Subscribe to at least one RV magazine. You'll be able to read about interesting places to go and things to see and do. "How-to" articles provide good information on improving, maintaining and repairing your rig. Technical and lifestyle experts respond to reader inquiries. Letters to the editor provide insight into the thoughts, complaints and quandaries of subscribers.

You'll also find the latest in RV books and other sources of information publicized or advertised in these magazines.

We recommend you subscribe to both a nationwide and a regional magazine. The nationwide will give you a broad perspective on the issues. The regional will provide you with information about camping destinations and RV services close to home.

Newspaper and Magazine Travel Sections - Although they may not be RV specific, many articles will be of interest to the RV traveler. Start saving those articles about places that interest you. We maintain a file folder for each state and refer to it when we are planning our travels.

RV Clubs - Join at least one nationwide RV club.
Among the largest are:
    Good Sam RV Owners Club (800-234-3450)
    Escapees RV Club (888-SKP-CLUB)
    Family Motor Coach Association (800-543-3622)
These RV clubs offer insurance programs, emergency roadside services and discounts at campgrounds. Membership also includes a periodic magazine with informative articles and columns.

Local RV clubs schedule weekend trips throughout the year. What better way to discover the campgrounds available in your area.

Brand name RV clubs are excellent sources of RV information and ideas. If you have a question about your RV, chances are that someone in that club who owns a similar model will know the answer.

Attend RV club rallies. They feature educational seminars by experts in every RV subject imaginable.

Automobile Clubs - The American Automobile Association, for example, is an excellent source for road maps and tour books. Members may also avail themselves of a trip routing service called Triptic. A Triptic is a series of loosely bound strip maps. They provide detailed information about the road, terrain and points of interest along your chosen route.

RV Accessory Store or Catalog - Most RV accessory stores will have a magazine and book rack. RV books not normally found in bookstores will be on display here. RV accessory catalogs offer RVing books and will keep you abreast of the latest in accessories and gadgets.

Libraries and Bookstores - It seems obvious, but many people overlook these treasure troves of information. Look under Camping, Motorhomes, Recreation, Recreation Vehicles and Travel Trailers. While you are there, look in the library's travel section for information on every state and tourist destination.

Computer Internet Web Sites - There are a variety of web sites offering information from RV manufacturers, dealers, campgrounds, clubs and more. An excellent starting point is our own **www.rvknowhow.com**

Computer On-line Services - Find out which online services offer RV forums. RV enthusiasts exchange experience, advice and ideas. RV manufacturers, dealers, service centers and publications participate in "discussions" and help with questions and problems.

Computer Software Stores - Mapping and travel software is available for computer owners. RVers can plot their trips based upon the quickest, shortest or most scenic route.

Government Travel and Camping Information - Contact the National Park Service, National Forest Service, U.S. Fish and Wildlife Service, Bureau of Land Management and U.S. Army Corps of Engineers for information about camping on public lands.

Check your campground directory for the address of each state's bureau of tourism. Send to them for state maps, campground directories and travel information.

County Parks and Recreation Departments, located in the county seat, can provide information about their county's camping opportunities.

Visitor Welcome Centers - Most states provide a visitor welcome center near their borders. Look for them in rest areas as you cross from one state to the next. Welcome centers will house racks of informative brochures placed there by commercial interests.

After perusing the brochure racks, go to the counter and ask for a state road map, state parks & campground directory and any other specialized information you can't find in the open. Often the best stuff is located behind the counter.

Travel Plazas (truck stops) - Travel plazas are courting the business of RV travelers. Some, like Flying J Travel Plazas, have even installed RV fuel islands for easy access. Visit their convenience stores and check out their magazine and book racks. You'll discover that the map and travel information needs of truckers is very similar to those of RVers.

Campground Stores - Their magazine, book and brochure racks may have information about RVs, RVing and local places of interest.

Campground Laundry Rooms - Here is where you get, firsthand, all the latest and the best information. RVers have a tendency to chat while waiting for their clothes to wash and dry. There's an excellent chance the person sharing the laundry room with you has just come from the direction you're heading. They can tell you their impressions of road conditions, campgrounds and attractions they have encountered. Some of our best tips and money-saving advice has come from people we've met in campground laundry rooms.

Enjoy The Journey!

Joe & Vicki Kieva

Visit our informative website: www.rvknowhow.com

Photo by Bill & Jan Moeller

About The Authors

Joe and Vicki Kieva refer to themselves as "RV Travel Junkies." During the last 40 years their journeys, in a variety of RVs, have taken them throughout the United States, Canada, Mexico and six European Countries.

In 1998, Joe and Vicki left their business careers to pursue a more enjoyable lifestyle, exploring America in an RV.

For a while they escorted RV caravans to Mexico and Alaska. Today, they criss-cross the country presenting RV lifestyle seminars at RV shows, rallies and educational events.

Joe and Vicki's seminars have made them popular figures in the RV community. They are probably best known, however, for their monthly RV advice columns in the Good Sam Club's *Highways* magazine and Woodall's *RV Traveler* publications

Between RV trips, Joe and Vicki reside in a house near their children and grandchildren in Huntington Beach, CA

More RV Books by Joe and Vicki Kieva
Read sample chapters on www.rvknowhow.com

RVing Made Easy - 184 Pages
How To Choose, Operate and Enjoy Your RV

Written in easy to understand, non-technical language.

You will learn:
- How to choose an RV that satisfies your interests and needs.
- How an RV's electrical, water and sewer systems work.
- How to equip, furnish and pack an RV.
- How to drive, back and level an RV.
- How to travel, locate campgrounds and select campsites.
- How to use an RV's hookup and self-containment features.
- How to cook, clean, do laundry, receive mail, make telephone calls, and fill prescriptions while on the road.

You're going to learn how easy RVing can be!

RVing Tips, Tricks & Techniques - 140 Pages
A Collection of RVing Articles by Joe and Vicki Kieva

Inside you will discover tips, tricks and techniques for:
- Simplifying Hookups
- Locating Dump Stations
- Dealing With Inclimate Weather
- Using Water Filters
- Controlling Holding Tank Odors
- Minimizing Condensation
- Deterring Insects and Critters

This book is a road map to making your dream a reality!

RVing Books by Joe and Vicki Kieva

RVing Made Easy
A non-technical book that helps you discover how easy it is to choose, operate, and enjoy your RV.

Extended RV Travel
Answers questions about choosing an RV, preparing for and living on the road for weeks/months at a time.

RVing Tips, Tricks And Techniques
This collection of Joe and Vicki Kieva's popular RV advice columns is a guide for successful RVing.

	Price	**Qty**	**Total**
RVing Made Easy	$16.95	_____	$_____
Extended RV Travel	$16.95	_____	$_____
RVing Tips, Tricks	$12.95	_____	$_____

Shipping – 1st book $3.00 (Canada $4.00 U.S.)
        Add $1.00 for each additional book $_____

                                         Subtotal $_____
      Calif. Residents add 7.75% sales tax $_____

Total (Please send check or money order in US funds) $_____

Your Name_____
  Address_____
    City_____ State _____ Zip _____

Mail to: RV Travel Adventures
              P.O. Box 5055
              Huntington Beach, Ca 92615